W9-AZZ-926

The
Going Lean
Fieldbook

The
Going Lean
Fieldbook

A Practical Guide to
Lean Transformation
and Sustainable Success

Stephen A. Ruffa

American Management Association

New York • Atlanta • Brussels • Chicago • Mexico City • San Francisco
Shanghai • Tokyo • Toronto • Washington, D.C.

Bulk discounts available. For details visit:
www.amacombooks.org/go/specialsales
Or contact special sales:
Phone: 800-250-5308
E-mail: specialsls@amanet.org
View all the AMACOM titles at: www.amacombooks.org

This publication is designed to provide accurate and authoritative information in regard to the subject matter covered. It is sold with the understanding that the publisher is not engaged in rendering legal, accounting, or other professional service. If legal advice or other expert assistance is required, the services of a competent professional person should be sought.

Library of Congress Cataloging-in-Publication Data

Ruffa, Stephen A., 1961–
    The going lean fieldbook : a practical guide to lean transformation and sustainable success / Stephen A. Ruffa. — 1st ed.
        p.   cm.
    Includes bibliographical references and index.
    ISBN-13: 978-0-8144-1558-0
    ISBN-10: 0-8144-1558-X
        1. Business logistics—Management.   2. Industrial efficiency.
    3. Organizational change.   I. Title.

    HD38.5.R844 2010
    658.5—dc22

                                        2010031663

© 2011 Lean Dynamics Research, LLC.
All rights reserved.
Printed in the United States of America.

This publication may not be reproduced, stored in a retrieval system, or transmitted in whole or in part, in any form or by any means, electronic, mechanical, photocopying, recording, or otherwise, without the prior written permission of AMACOM, a division of American Management Association, 1601 Broadway, New York, NY 10019.

About AMA
American Management Association (www.amanet.org) is a world leader in talent development, advancing the skills of individuals to drive business success. Our mission is to support the goals of individuals and organizations through a complete range of products and services, including classroom and virtual seminars, webcasts, webinars, podcasts, conferences, corporate and government solutions, business books and research. AMA's approach to improving performance combines experiential learning—learning through doing—with opportunities for ongoing professional growth at every step of one's career journey.

Printing number
10 9 8 7 6 5 4 3 2 1

For my wife, Staci,
and my children, Adam and Emily,
for their loving support.

CONTENTS

FOR SOME READERS, calling this a "fieldbook" will set the wrong expectation. To them, the term might imply a step-by-step guide to going lean; they might expect to find little more than a compilation of templates and checklists for implementing today's proliferation of discrete tools and activities whose direct application seems too often interpreted as the path to "leaning" the corporation.

The Going Lean Fieldbook does not follow this model.

Those who read my previous book, *Going Lean*, will recognize that such a focus would not make much sense. *Going Lean* showed that a much more complex context exists; that using a direct, "cookbook" approach for applying the techniques and practices made famous by Toyota is not the answer. It showed that what might succeed in gaining quick benefits amid simpler, steady conditions does not scale up well to address vast operations producing complex products within a dynamic environment.

The fundamental challenge extends beyond removing waste that is most visible—activities, delays, or materials that consume time and resources but do not contribute value—or mapping value streams, or applying techniques to improve standardization and orderliness. Instead, moving forward first requires taking a step back—taking a fresh look at the business conditions, the corporate mindset, and the management framework within the complex and sometimes chaotic environment in which one must operate—and then addressing the reasons these cause waste to accumulate in the first place.

In other words, going lean is not a matter of tweaking the status quo; it means completely rethinking the way business operates in order to advance within today's challenging conditions—the way Toyota began its efforts half a century ago.

Going Lean sparked a new way of looking at lean. Using examples backed by data, it showed why going lean means much more than excelling at day-to-day cost-cutting—the most frequent target of its tools and practices. Instead, it requires building dynamic capabilities that promote stability and consistency, even amid today's uncertain and ever-changing conditions, in order to make these outcomes possible. This means extending its application beyond the traditional limits of managing operations—promoting innovation and advancing broader strategic possibilities.

But such a view of lean—appropriately known as *lean dynamics* because it leads to very little waste and is highly responsive to change—also underscores the reality that a different path is needed. Lean dynamics raises new questions; for instance, how does one go about understanding the range of conditions that a company might face within today's dynamic environment? How well are individual corporations or public institutions equipped to deal with uncertainty and sudden change—and what changes will they need to make to meet these conditions? How can they adapt the costly improvements they might have already made, in order to fit them to this solution?

What managers, practitioners, educators, and workforces desperately need is a structured methodology, based on real cases, to sort through the complexities—a methodology that shows where they are, what direction they must go, and the specific actions that others have found to be important to making this transformation.

The Going Lean Fieldbook is intended to help. It offers a new model intended to fill this gaping void, building on the proven methods of lean manufacturing and the groundbreaking principles of lean dynamics first introduced in *Going Lean*. This book provides practical implementation ideas based on lessons from companies across different industries with different starting points and constraints. This information can help corporations and public institutions build a comprehensive lean strategy that overcomes even the most severe challenges and creates the sustainable excellence.

Intended as a companion book to *Going Lean*, this book can also serve as a stand-alone resource, a guide for grasping both theory and practical application. It offers a way for seeing through the rhetoric to understand the breadth of what is possible for businesses ranging from manufacturing, to medical, to government and even educational institutions. In conjunction with *Going Lean* it is intended to provide deeper insights into lean dynamics, helping people in different positions and with a range of backgrounds to recognize the urgent need for change that is critical for so many organizations today.

Beginning with a summary of the underlying principles of lean dynamics, *The Going Lean Fieldbook* highlights the series of levels corporations tend to attain as they mature through their journey toward lean dynamics transformation. Using specific cases and practical examples, it offers insights into creating a structured implementation approach leading to a critical and comprehensive dynamic strategy. It shows how integrating other methodologies and capabilities, from Six Sigma to information technology, can help, generating even greater potential for substantial, lasting benefits.

Simply stated, *The Going Lean Fieldbook* is intended as a tool to help businesses and institutions begin their successful journey to lean dynamics—a guide for understanding the range of challenges they must prepare to face in developing their path, starting from the various points in the current states of lean efforts. It can guide managers who are seeking to hire lean consulting firms by helping them understand which among the many "brands" of lean they wish to pursue, what goals to set, and how to measure progress and hold all involved accountable for results. And it can help guide an organization as it builds a strategy and methodology for proceeding on the journey to going lean—a critical but often neglected precursor to embarking on specific lean activities, which can define whether a lean effort will succeed.

The
Going Lean
Fieldbook

Solving the Problem with Lean

MORE THAN a decade and a half ago, I began my quest to understand what it takes for companies to succeed in going lean. After researching and demonstrating different applications for making its methods work, I became increasingly convinced that lean business practices offer a solution to the serious challenges so many corporations and institutions face today. I simply assumed that those engaged in implementation activities had grown in this belief as well and were solidly on board.

And then reality struck.

As I traveled the country following the release of *Going Lean*, I was astounded by reactions from people familiar with this term—that many who had been involved with it expressed outright disdain for anything termed *lean*. While I had previously understood that some misunderstanding likely existed, these frank discussions served as a rude awakening to the extent of their frustration.

How could this be? What was it that led so many people to stand so deeply against an approach that should instead inspire pride and optimism?

As I dug deeper, I ran across an interesting phenomenon. Despite lean's enormous popularity among executives and practitioners,

1

I found that a tremendous divide often exists between them and those in the workforce and even within the ranks of middle management—with the former often completely unaware of the feelings of the latter. I began to study this disconnect; it seemed clear that overcoming it would be critical to fostering advancement of a system so dependent on those very people for its success.

Then it hit me. For years I had been closely following and contributing to the advancements in understanding lean as a principle-based approach founded on solid theory and a rigorous structure for implementation. What I had missed was that its *implementation* had very often taken a different course altogether.

Too many firms and institutions seem to be chasing the latest fads rather than implementing rigorous programs founded on the accumulation of decades of knowledge. Attention goes to the individual tools and techniques—often without much focus on the deeper, transformational aspects that lean methods were intended to advance. And the result has become all too clear: serious inconsistencies in how lean is being approached—and, along with this, an alarmingly high level of frustration.

Moreover, I found that the term *lean* no longer brings to mind a single approach; companies and institutions have flocked to its growing number of variants (sometimes as a way to escape its Japanese jargon and unyielding production-based structure). Depending on which of these a business or an institution begins with, lean might assume a very different structure and methodology. These varying interpretations of what lean is all about appear to have contributed to confusion and frustration, and to the very different levels of understanding, maturity, and plateaus in performance that corporations and institutions seem to attain.

So what, then, *is* lean?

On the surface, the answer seems quite obvious. Lean implies the opposite of bloated; going lean therefore suggests cutting out the fat— taking direct aim at operational waste in all its forms and thereby slashing corporations' cost of doing business. Companies focus on removing excess inventories, unneeded movement, and unnecessary processing steps. They apply it alongside technology solutions for improving information, and couple it with Six Sigma for driving down defects. In all, lean has become synonymous with cutting down the time, materials, and effort it takes to get things done.

Yet, within today's complex, dynamic business world, this is not nearly enough.

Why is this? While the term *lean* is powerfully descriptive of the *outcomes* this approach represents, implementing improvement in a way that directly targets these outcomes is not the answer. Doing so leaves the foundation supporting how a firm or an institution should roll out its efforts largely unaddressed. Worse still, most charge ahead without first acknowledging their *dynamic conditions*—those shifts in customer demands or changing business circumstances that cause disruption and drive this "waste" to accumulate in the first place. In doing so, organizations risk trivializing what lean is really all about and falling seriously short of attaining lasting improvement.[1]

The Dynamic Basis for Lean

Eliminating operational excess has long been the Holy Grail of American business. Henry Ford's Model T was perhaps the clearest example of its application—a powerful demonstration of the cost reduction made possible by precisely honing work steps. But *how* this is done is of critical importance. History shows that Henry Ford optimized his methods for the largely stable environment in which he operated at the time.[2] However, such stability could not last. When Ford's business was ultimately forced to adapt to customers' increasing demands for variety, the company's fortunes precipitously declined.[3]

Many of today's corporations maintain a similar focus. Founded on management principles that were honed during the industrial boom throughout the early part of the twentieth century, many companies operate largely on a presumption of stability—a belief that customer's demands will remain consistent and predictable; that conditions will remain inherently reliable. This belief in strong, consistent demand broken infrequently by short periods of adjustment has driven the widespread practices of optimizing for economies of scale and managing-by-outcomes that still dominate businesses of all types. Manufacturers, airlines, retailers, medical providers, educational institutions, and others align their operations, organize their departments, structure their information systems, and plan the introduction of new products and services within a mindset of optimizing for the specific range of conditions they currently face.

Such a mindset, however, can leave them largely unprepared for the longer, more dramatic shifts that today have become the norm. Economic downturns, spikes in oil prices, and fallout from catastrophic events can quickly erode any gains from "leaning" out activities; companies might see their cost savings quickly erode, their "wastes" reemerge, and their hard-earned quality and efficiencies wane (a result that recent events have so broadly demonstrated). Moreover, many of the changes that companies make to optimize their processes during stable times can instead increase the turmoil and waste that result when uncertainty spikes and conditions suddenly change.

But if going lean is not about "cutting the fat," what is it? Answering this requires that we first understand the driving reasons behind why the widely regarded benchmark for lean manufacturing, the Toyota Motor Corporation, began its journey toward lean.

A Foundation in Crisis

Toyota began its foray into lean manufacturing soon after the end of World War II as a means for overcoming what must have seemed to be overwhelming constraints. Struggling to gain a foothold despite low, volatile demand for its products (the worst possible mix for a manufacturer), Toyota had to compete with the likes of Detroit, which was thriving amid predictable, expanding mass markets. Moreover, Toyota had to deal with a labor revolt that forced it to make unprecedented agreements to get the workforce back into its factories— including the guarantee of lifelong employment.4

What could the company do? Traditional methods clearly could not overcome these challenges, which were far more severe than its competitors had to deal with. Hiring and firing its people to adjust for changes in demand were no longer the answer. Instead, Toyota applied a new way of thinking, shifting everything from how it performed work to the way it shared information and made decisions—even how it rolled out innovation. And in doing so, it created the means for turning what had now become its most valuable asset—its work-force—into a powerful competitive advantage.

The company broke from the traditional practice of separating work into repetitive processing steps and then synchronizing these using top-down controls. Instead, it created autonomous teams with sufficient skills and equipment to turn out *product families* (groups of items sharing similar processing characteristics)—producing entire parts or components from beginning to end. This made it possible to more precisely synchronize each of its activities with the actual needs of its customers—*pulling* just what was needed to match their rate of consumption at each step rather than *pushing* materials along to meet preset schedules.

Toyota factories no longer produced and stored enormous batches of identical items with the objective of optimizing for a narrow range of anticipated conditions to attain large *economies of scale*. Instead, they turned out smaller quantities that much more closely represented actual customer demand at each step of production. This created the powerful effect of leveling out uncertainty and disruption across the supply chain and, in doing so, generating a different kind of efficiency that more than offset the great economies of scale that traditional practices could produce.

Toyota developed a range of tools and techniques to make this work, supporting such advancements as rapid changeovers for shifting from producing one configuration to the next (a key to gaining the benefits needed from its product family approach, as described in Chapter 6). The result is a system of management that is much better suited to the dynamic business conditions that have today become the norm.

But it is important to understand that Toyota does not stand alone. Airlines like Southwest Airlines, other manufacturers, and even Walmart adopted this very different way of managing their business as they, too, grew facing tremendous challenges. And, like Toyota, they go far beyond targeting the visible outcomes of speedier operations and reduced "waste" so commonly seen as the reasons for their success. By applying a common set of principles, or *lean dynamics*, their lessons point to a powerful means for overcoming the forces of uncertainty and change and, in doing so, achieving excellence across a broad range of conditions.

Structuring for Lean Dynamics

Going Lean first described the concept of lean dynamics, introducing a clear way to identify those who have succeeded in applying the tools and practices of lean manufacturing to flexibly respond to changes in customer demand, environmental shifts, and other factors. By pinpointing which firms stand above the rest in responding to the shifting conditions and changing demands of today's dynamic business environment, and identifying their shared characteristics, it isolated the principles key to their strong, sustained performances over time.

How is it possible to identify such firms? By using the *value curve*—a graphical tool that illustrates how well an organization creates value within an environment of change. Lean dynamics firms display a stark, distinct difference from traditionally managed companies. They yield stronger, steadier, tangible value even across the most severe market conditions.

Consider the implications. Despite facing serious challenges—from the aftermath of September 11, 2001, to hurricane Katrina, and later when oil prices spiked to near historic levels—these companies continued to advance. Not only did they demonstrate the capability to seamlessly shift their activities and deliberately respond to changing business needs, their much greater flexibility made it less disruptive to roll out new innovations. Their results made it clear that they had gone well beyond the traditional objective of increasing efficiency; instead they demonstrated a dynamic capability to apply business strategies suited to anticipating and responding to changing conditions—even transforming customers' expectations in a way that promoted their own ability to respond.

This fundamentally different way of viewing lean points to a very different starting point. A lean dynamics program *does not directly target waste elimination*; rather, it focuses on the underlying reasons why waste accumulates in the first place—identifying and addressing disconnects across the business that cause the need for buffers, delays, and workarounds, which amplify internal disruption, create *lag*, and increase loss when conditions change. This focus is critical to structuring a program for improvement that goes beyond trimming operational costs and, instead, builds stability and sustained excellence. Without first addressing major disconnects, localized improvements might simply fade away over time, displaced by disruption, workarounds, and waste that reemerges once conditions inevitably shift.

Just as important is mitigating the severe impact this disruption can have on innovation—a critical force for inspiring customers to buy in the first place. For traditionally managed companies, the challenge is clear. Introducing the latest technology into fresh new products or services can force significant changes in a company's activities—everything from factory layout, work procedures, equipment, and even suppliers—amplifying variation and potentially driving widespread disruption and loss to lagging operations. Mitigating this lag is important to overcoming what can become a deep-seated resistance to introducing new value—a reluctance to press forward with new products and services because of the disruption this would cause, even when there exists a clear demand.

Yet the most immediate focus must be on identifying and correcting those disconnects that act as barriers to engaging the workforce in a meaningful way, thus eliminating a cause for alienation that frequently occurs early in a transformation. The answer cannot come from slogans or management dictates; these cannot impart the genuine enthusiasm that has proven so important for success. Only through restructuring activities so that individuals across the business can become meaningfully involved will they come to understand not only the compelling need for change but develop a deep appreciation of how they must contribute.

Driving a Shared Sense of Purpose

While *Going Lean* comprehensively described the *what*—the principles, tools, and practices of lean dynamics—there remains considerable disagreement on *how* to best apply them. Still, leaders of major improvement activities of all sorts do seem to agree on one point: There exists a critical need for gaining broad-based understanding and buy-in by the workforce.

One widely recognized method for building such support is to pursue low-hanging fruit by beginning with the most straightforward targets in order to demonstrate rapid gains. Such a mindset seems particularly prominent within organizations set on going lean; individuals who become trained in uncovering hidden wastes naturally seek to drive out as much inefficiency as possible and thus demonstrate quick savings.

And, as a result, many have missed the mark.

I have often listened in frustration to managers who proudly tout case after case of waste reduction success—while appearing painfully unaware of the widespread disdain for their efforts that has grown among the workforce. Despite participating in continuous improvement activities deliberately structured to promote employee inclusion, many workers continue to feel alienated from what they regard as a top-down directive. I am often astounded by the number of people who have come to regard going lean as a real problem; people from various levels across a wide range of corporations and institutions have bluntly shared with me their distaste for this "fad." How can this be, particularly with so much effort and attention aimed at the workforce?

Much of the problem, it seems, boils down to a context for implementation that trivializes its intent, causing many to misinterpret lean as "something we should have been doing anyway," or as nothing more than a repackaging of "failed techniques of the past." And companies too often reinforce this perception by bypassing critical steps in their eagerness to quickly engage their workforce.

For instance, within large, complex, diverse businesses, lean efforts frequently seem to begin with targeted exercises that seek to create quick wins. Often these consist of facilitated exercises using "sticky notes" with which teams tag wasteful steps or identify changes to improve the cleanliness and orderliness of their work areas. While each of these do have a place, their stand-alone application seems to promote an oversimplified perception of lean, perhaps causing more harm than good.

Engaging the workforce in improvement initiatives requires adequately preparing workers and then including them in meaningful activities for building a solid foundation for their success. However, workers should not be asked to identify improvements affecting the progression of complex activities spanning vast corporations when they possess only a fragmented understanding of the business. Corporations must first create a framework that substantially broadens workers', managers', and even suppliers' *span of insight*, expanding their understanding of how their work fits into the business's broader objectives and constraints.

For most organizations, this requires some degree of restructuring—dismantling the compartmentalization that has for so long caused departments, workstations, and individuals to optimize for the purpose of their own disparate objectives. This takes structuring improvements by breaking down traditional functional barriers, decentralizing authority, and sharing information to create greater insight into the bottom-line meaning and impact of each step along the way (described in Chapter 6). All must gain a clearer, shared understanding of what goes into creating value from end to end across the business—how each step they perform will create direct value to the customer and contribute to well understood objectives.

Overcoming the challenges that have undermined so many efforts comes not only from learning from those who have long since attained sustainable excellence but from piecing together the best lessons of those still working toward this goal. Perhaps most important is studying their progress as organizations face the challenges of a severe, uncertain business environment—conditions that today are not hard to find.

Lean as a Means for Conquering Crisis

Going Lean was published in 2008, when one of the largest business crises this country has ever experienced began to unfold. An economic tsunami hit companies large and small, sweeping indiscriminately across industries of all types. Corporations quickly found themselves caught in its wake, with many succumbing to what soon became regarded as the most challenging environment in nearly a century.

As the downturn progressed, a simple question came to mind: What lessons can be learned about lean dynamics in the midst of this extraordinary environment?

As it turned out, firms described or identified in *Going Lean* for their sustained excellence (including Southwest Airlines, Walmart, Hibbett Sports) continued to perform strongly, even advancing as competitors struggled. Almost all sustained a profit (with the notable exception of Toyota, which sustained less of a financial loss compared to major competitors that required tens of billions of dollars in government bailouts—although it struggled through serious quality problems, apparently the result of an unfortunate shift from its former focus, discussed in Chapter 10). Most continued to press forward, operating largely as they had done before, sustaining their businesses in a way that seems to position them to surge forward when business conditions eventually improve.

Just as important was what this crisis revealed about companies that had been in the midst of their lean journeys. In researching this book, I reached out to a range of organizations and gathered available information on others to better understand what they had done. Some had established techniques to overcome specific challenges; others had built powerful enabling tools. Many offered compelling lessons in implementing different aspects of the concepts that had been identified in *Going Lean*. Still others had shown evidence of what *not* to do; for instance, that conducting widespread but unguided improvement exercises could undermine workforce support—a key challenge to progressing toward sustainable results.

This book serves to pull these findings together. It captures the powerful lessons of companies of varying sizes and types across different industries in their advancement toward lean *maturity*; in doing so, it provides a means for distinguishing between initiatives offering only temporary improvement and those important to progressing toward sustainable excellence.

What do these lessons show? This book explains that advancement begins by learning to see the gaps in traditional methods, but that the path to lean does not directly target the problem. Rather than first addressing the processes where waste is observed, firms and institutions need to take a step back and reassess the way they have chosen to assemble value. Moreover, they need to shift from a mindset of unguided continuous improvement to instead identifying and successively addressing *focal points for structuring their transformation—*

a shift that holds potential to dramatically impact their effectiveness in advancing within the complexities of a dynamic environment.

A lean dynamics solution seeks to prioritize action in these areas as part of a broad methodology for increasing capabilities and progressively advancing in lean maturity. Doing so serves as a means for extending the workforce's insight and involvement, putting them in the driver's seat for addressing pressing customer and business needs, while paving the way for new opportunities to meet the emerging needs of the future.

How to Use This Book

The Going Lean Fieldbook offers a structure for gauging an organization's starting point and for assessing where it should begin, from wherever it currently stands in its lean journey. Illustrated by real cases and practical examples, this book identifies a series of levels that mark organizations' journey to lean maturity, providing the broader context needed for setting a winning course while preventing the misunderstandings that can lead to false starts. Corporations can begin down this path by setting the comprehensive, dynamic, and specific strategy that is critical, yet missing from so many efforts today, which integrates the following core elements:

- **Insight:** Create and sustain a shared sense of purpose, a clear and compelling case for change, and objectives and metrics that are understood and embraced at all levels and across the enterprise.

- **Inclusion:** Shift from a system driven by top-down control and outcome-based measures to one that draws on increasing insights, capabilities, and authority of the workforce, enabling direct accountability and visibility of value creation at each step in its buildup.

- **Action:** Relentlessly eliminate lag as a critical means to driving down waste and attaining strong, steady customer and corporate value across a broad range of conditions.

◼ **Integration:** Build a structure for organizing, guiding, tracking, and synchronizing transformation activities across the enterprise.

This book is not intended to serve as a replacement for case studies or textbooks that hone in with greater detail on individual tools and practices. Instead, it should act as a guide for implementing the underlying principles they describe. It offers a framework for evaluating organizations' current vision and assessing their dynamic value creation—important steps for creating their own lean dynamics roadmap to success. Perhaps most importantly, it points the way to gaining workforce buy-in—often the single greatest challenge and most important element to its successful implementation.

The book is organized into three parts. The first describes how lean dynamics is different and why its philosophy and principles are critical to gaining a competitive edge in today's business world. The second presents core elements that define its application, describing different ways of applying widely recognized lean tools and techniques to develop powerful capabilities that support sustainable results. The third completes the picture, presenting a methodology for constructing a lean dynamics solution and insights derived from a range of complex industries whose efforts offer lessons on individual elements.

Each chapter highlights one or more of three types of supporting information for applying its contents, as follows:

Key Point: Emphasizes specific aspects of points within a chapter considered important to understanding a concept central to implementation

Caution: Identifies critical challenges that might derail lean dynamics efforts

Case Example: Provides insights into how concepts described within a chapter were applied in a specific situation to deepen understanding into how they might relate to other circumstances

The book concludes with appendices that describe a framework for two central concepts within the lean dynamics transformation. Appendix A discusses steps for conducting the dynamic value assessment and summarizes supporting portions of the book; it is envisioned as both an executive summary and a resource for practitioners to refer back to while implementing lean dynamics projects. Appendix B describes the construction of the value curve—a central tool that supports the shift to lean dynamics—and the application of its elements as part of a lean dynamics program.

By suggesting a framework and strategy to proceed, supported by these key points, cautions, and cases, *The Going Lean Fieldbook* is intended to help corporations and institutions of all types through the most critical and challenging part of their lean journeys: the starting point. Moreover, it is hoped that showing how all lean efforts are not alike will help firms and institutions adopt a deliberate methodology for advancing toward the ultimate level of lean maturity, creating strong, sustainable corporate and customer value that can withstand the test of time.

PART

1 A Case for Change

B EFORE ONE EMBARKS on a complex journey, it is fair to ask the simple questions: Why not just stay put? What is wrong with the status quo, and how much will really be gained by stepping forward onto this difficult road? After all, it is human nature to cling to the comfort of what is known and resist the challenges and uncertainty of what might lie ahead. The more risky the traveler perceives the journey to be, the more likely that he or she will not venture far from home—which means never reaching the intended destination.

Chapter 1 makes clear the basic reason that there no longer remains much choice but to venture ahead. It describes how today's environment of uncertainty and change is undermining many corporations' and institutions' ability to succeed. It explains why merely tweaking what they do now is no longer an option; why sustaining business excellence will take adopting a different focus to better anticipate and more effectively respond to this growing challenge.

Chapter 2 describes the rationale and foundation for making a case for this change to the leadership, employees, and key stakeholders. It describes a new approach for identifying "value," and assessing how well a business or an institution is suited to delivering strong, consistent value across the range of conditions it might face. This is an important step to fostering the understanding, buy-in, and sense of excitement that is critical yet very often neglected.

Chapter 3 concludes this part by examining the road ahead for those beginning their lean journey. It describes the five levels of lean maturity and the reasons why firms often stagnate along the way. Finally, it shows that advancing in lean maturity requires a vision, structure, and specific techniques for overcoming the potential to stagnate.

Redefining the Competitive Solution

"**W**E'RE HERE TODAY because we made mistakes," CEO Rick Wagoner said to the congressional committee. "And because some forces beyond our control have pushed us to the brink."[1]

With this simple statement, the leader of General Motors—once the world's most powerful manufacturer—essentially acknowledged defeat. The company found itself on the edge of disaster; it could remain afloat only if Congress agreed to give it tens of billions of dollars in taxpayer-funded bailouts—and even then its survival was anything but assured.

How could this titan of manufacturing have plunged into such crisis? Sure, the economy had suffered its worst decline in nearly a century. And with it, customers had simply stopped buying. Yet congressional critics addressed Wagoner and his counterparts at Ford and Chrysler with the same criticism voiced by many observers— that before this downturn, Detroit had been in a steady decline for several decades. Now this once dominant corporation—along with much of this country's automotive industry—teetered at the brink of extinction.

What went wrong with GM and so many other corporations? Have America's businesses become soft, unable to see the inefficiencies and waste that crept into their operations? Is their challenge as clear as many describe: Find a way to stretch their business further—demand more from workers, speed up processes, apply greater information technology, or outsource more work to lower wage regions? Does the secret to sustaining competitive advantage boil down to finding a better way of cutting costs?

Like so many of America's other once mighty corporations, it appears that GM had simply fallen victim to its own success. For decades, the company's unquestioned market leadership gave it little reason to really change. Despite valiant efforts aimed at cutting costs and refining its methods, it seems that the company did so within the confines of its traditional framework for doing business—an approach that proved to be not nearly enough.

The unfortunate reality is that the environment in which this company must operate today looks dramatically different from the one for which its business practices were built nearly a century ago. Despite all the rationalization and finger pointing, this basic disconnect has significantly contributed to its long, dramatic decline. And this is the same challenge that so many of this nation's corporations and institutions face as well.

Seeing Beyond Stability

GM's way of doing business traces back to its historic quest early last century to achieve the unthinkable. In 1921 the company's newly appointed president, Alfred Sloan, set out to break Henry Ford's iron-clad lock on the automotive industry—one that he held for nearly two decades. Sloan recognized that the enormous efficiencies Ford's methods generated made competing head-to-head based on low pricing a losing proposition. So Sloan pointed his company in a very different direction—restructuring for a business environment that he sensed had undergone a substantial shift.

With automobiles becoming widely available, Sloan recognized that customers no longer sought rock-bottom pricing as their only consideration. He built a system that moved beyond Ford's approach of driving down costs by producing huge quantities of nearly identical vehicles. As described in *Going Lean*, Sloan instead set out to promote a "mass-class" market, which encouraged more people to buy better and better cars—something that Ford's way of doing business was ill-suited to support.[2]

GM succeeded in bringing variety and choice within reach of its customers, moving beyond Ford's presumption of a single product mass market in favor of a strategy of variety. With five lines of vehicles, its offerings could meet a broad range of customer needs and financial capabilities. This strategy succeeded; it ultimately launched GM to dominate what became the largest manufacturing industry in the world.

Sloan managed his company by operating under what he called *coordinated control of decentralized operations*.[3] This meant that the company's different divisions operated as separate, distinct organizations—designing and producing different lines of vehicles while generating economies of scale through many of their shared resources. But with it came a new burden: the challenge of managing the incredible complexity this created. He needed a way to simplify the problem—to look at each part of the business in the same way, but while preserving the distinct character of each division that would drive his strategy's success.

What he came up with was a means to track performance by smoothing out short-term fluctuations, essentially measuring based on *average* production levels, something he called *standard volume*.[4] This greatly simplified oversight, making it easier to relate costs to their driving factors and determine where greater attention was needed, such as where to focus to maximize workforce, inventory, and equipment efficiencies and which managers were performing well relative to forecasted expectations.

It also made it possible to structure the business in a way that gave managers the insights they needed for maintaining efficient use of people, facilities, and equipment without tracking the myriad of details that had made Henry Ford's methods so complex. Managers no longer focused on the individual details of work as products progressed down the line. Instead, they set their sights on optimizing factories for the averages, which meant turning out huge batches of identical items at a rate that approximated standard volumes. The downside was that efficiencies dropped off precipitously if they had to operate outside of their intended production conditions.

For a long time, this same basic management system thrived; its underlying presumption of steady, predictable demand seemed to closely match the reality of prevailing business conditions. Industries of all types embraced it as the gold standard for managing complex businesses. Today, however, its limitations are becoming increasingly clear, causing an effect that has become quite serious.

To understand why, let us look to an analogous situation that most readers recently experienced in their own lives. The summer of 2008 brought with it a challenge that many people had never before experienced. Gasoline prices rapidly increased, rocketing beyond the dreaded $3-per-gallon threshold and quickly exceeding $4 per gallon. The impact was immediate and crippling, with people everywhere struggling to pay what had become exorbitant amounts simply to fuel their cars.

Americans faced a growing crisis. But what was the cause? Surprisingly, as clear as it seemed, the issue was not simply the high price at the pump. Instead, unaffordable gasoline was merely the visible symptom of a much deeper issue—a dangerous condition that had been quietly developing for years.

The "Steady-State" Trap

Many years ago I began a weekly routine of fueling my car in preparation for my drive to work on the days ahead. I clearly recall the price. Gasoline cost somewhere around a dollar and a quarter per gallon. More than two decades later I distinctly remember noting that not much had changed; the price of gasoline still fell within the dollar-something range.

The presumption of such steady fuel prices factored heavily into the choices I made (not necessarily consciously)—just as it seemed to for many others. The result was significant and widespread: suburbs grew rapidly, as did the size of the typical vehicle. Americans' average daily commute increased substantially, while trucks and SUVs increasingly filled the highways. It is not hard to see why Americans broke record after record for their consumption of huge quantities of low-cost gasoline.

And in doing so, people everywhere locked themselves into lifestyles that were increasingly dependent on continued price stability.

And then everything changed.

When gasoline prices suddenly spiked, most people could do little to change. They still had to drive to work, and they still had to take care of the many obligations that depended on their use of gasoline. The difference was that fuel was no longer inexpensive; drivers everywhere suddenly had to make tough choices in response to their ever-tightening financial circumstances. And the result soon spread to the broader economy.

America's corporations face much the same challenge. Consider the sales trend in the automotive industry, depicted in Figure 1-1. The left side of the graph depicts a smooth and predictable demand pattern in the years following World War II (shown in terms of overall sales)—precisely the environment for which Sloan's sys-

Figure 1-1. Automotive Industry Demand Shift

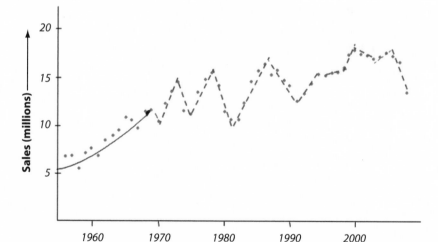

Data Source: Sales from 1965 to 2008: *Ward's Motor Vehicles Facts & Figures 2009*, a publication of Ward's Automotive Group, Southfield, MI USA.
Sales for 1956 to 1964: *MVMA Motor Vehicle Facts & Figures*, Motor Vehicle Manufacturers Association of the United States, Inc.[5]

tem of management was intended. And for decades, this environment persisted; businesses and institutions everywhere came to operate well within a remarkably narrow range of largely predictable conditions.

In the early 1970s, the environment abruptly shifted. Unpredictability skyrocketed; customers' interests began to shift. Businesses that had structured themselves based on a presumption of stability—operating at or near narrowly optimized rates to create great economies of scale to meet precisely forecasted customer needs—suddenly found themselves locked into a way of doing business that was ill-suited for these very different conditions. And each new bout of disruption brought with it the same result: workarounds, disruption, and crisis.

What is particularly striking is how closely this shift correlates to the timeframe in which Detroit's reputation—along with its market share—began its steep decline. This should have served as a wake-up call for the challenges American producers would face. Yet rather than making a fundamental change to accommodate these dramatically different conditions, they redoubled efforts to stretch their existing product focus and practices a little further—and in doing so achieved the same basic result.

Why does this create such a problem? *Going Lean* described that such unstable conditions cause substantial internal *variation*—deviations from intended plans, objectives, or outcomes within traditionally managed organizations built for stability. Variation leads to operational unpredictability, driving the need for workarounds, inventories, and other buffers—*waste* that draws corporate resources without contributing to creating customer value.

Key Point: What Is Waste?

The late Taiichi Ohno, a recognized architect of the famed Toyota Production System, identified seven forms of waste—excesses that do not add value but draw resources, attention, and create delay and overreaction that promotes more waste.[6]

1. **Overproduction** is caused when manufacturers build large quantities of items to maximize economies of scale or build large inventories to buffer against uncertain or changing demands.

2. **Waiting** is a frequent result of shortages, equipment failures, or other causes of delay from a system suffering the disruptive effects of operational discontinuities.

3. **Transportation** is one of the more visible forms of waste, including long travel distances that create the potential for delay and the need to handle material several times during delivery or receipt.

4. **Processing** waste includes extra steps that can creep in over time in dealing with recurring challenges like defects, shortages, and delays due to lagging, disconnected work, or flawed information.

5. **Inventory** waste is most apparent when manufacturers maintain large quantities of either end items or work-in-progress as a way to bridge value-creating activities whose flow is otherwise disconnected or uncertain.

6. **Motion** that takes time but does not contribute to the result is wasteful, such as workers searching for tools or "chasing parts" to prevent stoppages from stock-outs.

7. **Defects** are wasteful on multiple levels. They must be corrected, distracting from operations and causing work that does not create value. Removal of defective parts can cause material shortages on a production line, leading to several other forms of waste (waiting, transportation, motion). Frequent defects create uncertainty, which drives an increase in inventory, another form of waste.

Removing these excesses has become a primary target of today's cost-conscious managers. Yet waste (along with the variation that can drive its necessity) can be difficult and expensive to control—often it simply recurs once conditions again shift. Moreover, attacking waste directly can backfire, creating localized gains with little impact on the bottom line while compromising firms' abilities to make more meaningful progress.

The real answer is to implement a solution that helps corporations and institutions better respond to change by restructuring to address *lag*—the real driver that acts to amplify this variation and drive up *loss* in customer and corporate value.

Solving the Problem of Lag

A key takeaway from *Going Lean* is that stable, predictable operating conditions can no longer be the central assumption of American business. What distinguishes truly lean corporations is their very different way of doing business that lets them perform consistently and effectively across a wide range of circumstances.

What exactly do the benchmarks of lean dynamics show? Although the reasons for their success are often explained through their many distinct characteristics and practices, the real answer is much more fundamental. They simply function with far less lag to amplify variation and disruption during changing business circumstances. This lets them quickly adapt, even meeting shifts head-on with innovative solutions—turning what others see as crises into opportunities for advancement.

But what exactly *is* lag? Lag is delay caused by discontinuities within a system; these act to amplify uncertainty and disruption, impacting the creation of value. To better understand this, think of the lagging response we have all probably faced when we adjust the temperature of our shower, an analogous situation described by MIT professor Peter Senge in his book *The Fifth Discipline*:

> After you turn up the heat, the water remains cold. You receive no
> response to your action, so you perceive that your act has had no effect.
> You respond by continuing to turn up the heat. When the hot water finally
> arrives, a 190-degree water gusher erupts from the faucet. You jump out
> and turn it back, and, after another delay, it's frigid again.[7]

In much the same way, activities that are riddled with large inventories, extended schedules, and long travel distances tend to amplify the effects of uncertainty. The lag these discontinuities create typically goes unnoticed when business remains steady and reliable. However, demand spikes or other sudden shifts ultimately lead to an exaggerated response that creates disruption and delay, causing customer value to rapidly degrade and waste to accumulate.

Consider the reaction to a sudden shift in production within a traditionally managed factory. Individuals performing compartmentalized functions typically have little warning of the changes before they strike. Ad hoc actions take over; workarounds quickly displace tightly synchronized plans, causing disruption to spread up and down the supplier chain. Defects and missed deliveries become rampant, while costs skyrocket. Each unforeseen change brings the need for new workarounds—added inventories and schedule padding, or more people and steps to facilitate expediting—most of which remain in place long after the crisis has passed. Over time these wastes accumulate, drawing ever-increasing resources while adding further to the underlying disconnects that are at the root of this challenge.

Correcting lag that causes this downward spiral of loss is what lean dynamics is all about. This book explains why doing so requires a logical, structured approach that progressively addresses the complex interrelationship between each of the major types of flow: operational, organizational, information, and innovation. The result includes not only achieving the lean outcomes that corporations typically seek to attain—greater quality, innovation, and operational efficiencies—but, most importantly, enabling new business strategies while mitigating the impact of dynamic conditions.

Key Point: Recognizing the Impact of Lag

A central tenet of lean dynamics is to address the lag that creates disruptive outcomes when businesses are subjected to uncertainty and change. This lag can come from disconnects between measurement and outcome, often the result of gaps in the flow of information, work activities, or decisions. The best way to understand the cycle of loss this creates is by thinking of how lag impacts each of the four primary forms of flow.

1. **Operational flow** is what we often think of when we picture the buildup of value—the progression of those activities involved in transforming products or services from their basic elements to their finished state, delivered into the hands of the customer. For traditional operations, smooth flow comes from precisely synchronizing inventories and activities to meet steady conditions. But when demand suddenly spikes, for instance, inventories can be depleted and schedule buffers overrun, causing shortages that disrupt standardization and synchronization across the business. The underlying disconnects become exposed, but not before amplifying disruption and crisis until operations finally stabilize at a state of loss that can be many times greater than before.

2. **Organizational flow** is characterized by the smooth progression of decision making by people at all levels and points across the creation of value, which prevents misdirection or overreaction to changes. Organizational structures designed to operate smoothly under normal conditions can quickly shift when crisis strikes. Steep hierarchical structures and strong functional divisions limit individuals' span of insight, which can amplify disruption when conditions change. The result can be delay followed by misdirection—missing the real issue or correcting problems with a sledgehammer that, with earlier intervention, might have been resolved with only a small tap.

3. **Information flow** works closely with operational and organizational flow in creating the smooth movement of accurate, timely information to the right people at all levels and points across the creation of value. Information systems seek to improve flow by sharing insights, just as a traffic report alerts drivers about disruptions ahead. Still, the best information can only do so much; a traffic report does little good if there are no exits from the highway. And treating these systems as a stand-alone solution can *increase* lag.

4. **The flow of innovation** can be seriously impacted within firms riddled with lag. The introduction of new products or services forces significant changes, which create variation

that can disrupt operational flow, particularly where buffers or other lagging factors are present. Corporations tend to avoid this by regulating innovation–extending their existing products and services as long as possible, replacing them only when the loss from making this change is clearly outweighed by the urgent need to generate new sales–something that makes little sense for competing in today's hypercompetitive global marketplace.

Approaching Lean as a Dynamic Business Solution

Just weeks after the tragedy of September 11, 2001, I arrived at one of the nation's busiest airports on my way to a conference. I was shocked by what I saw—what was usually a beehive of activity was virtually empty. Besides those who were working there, I saw few other people throughout the entire terminal.

The implications for the U.S. airline industry were enormous. The bottom had completely fallen out—people everywhere simply stopped flying. Most of the airlines responded to the sudden drop in demand the same way. Without passengers to fill their seats, they cancelled flights and grounded as much as a quarter of their fleet. Employees were either furloughed or laid off in droves. Despite taking such drastic measures, all of the major carriers suffered dramatic losses—with many ultimately falling into bankruptcy.

That is, except one.

In the midst of this crisis that shook at the industry's foundation, Southwest Airlines stood apart. It did not react to the severe downturn and other events following this crisis as its competitors had done. The company kept all of its planes in the air; its employees all remained on the job.[8] And it was the only major airline to profit.

How was this possible? Because Southwest Airlines' way of doing business is not governed by the conventional system described earlier in this chapter. Whereas others had structured their businesses based on maximizing economies of scale—a way of doing business intended for profiting in a steady, predictable mass market—Southwest Airlines had gone a different direction entirely. As the company's founder and former CEO, Herb Kelleher, put it: "Market share has nothing to do with profitability."9 Instead, it seems, Southwest focuses on turning out steady value, no matter how conditions change.

By creating a strong connection between what its customers want and its own ability to efficiently operate, the company can quickly adjust to even dramatic changes in its environment. Its steady operations, decision making, information, and even innovation in the face of this and other challenges that followed demonstrate that this company's approach stands apart from the rest.

Southwest Airlines is not alone; large and small companies (described in Chapter 9) within a range of industries also demonstrate that sustained business excellence demands a different focus. Despite their very different challenges and constraints, these companies display the following set of shared characteristics, which point the way for others to follow:10

Preparing for Uncertainty and Change

Firms that demonstrate lean dynamics consistently display an uncanny preparedness for change—even crisis. Their long histories of overcoming serious challenges seem to have given them a deep recognition that change and uncertainty are here to stay. Those who wish to follow in their path must develop a similar focus: They must develop the ability to thrive across a broad range of circumstances, steadily advancing their capabilities for delivering consistent, ever-increasing customer and corporate value.

But what *is* value? For these firms the meaning seems quite clear: Value is simply *what their customers say it is—even if they continue to change their minds.* This means that value is not static in nature; rather, it is constantly evolving, driven by changing technologies, competitive forces, and customer desires.

Satisfying this demand for *dynamic* value means seeking to understand, and even anticipate, customers' needs and to satisfy them by constantly developing and rolling out new innovations—not just when existing offerings have run their course. It requires developing the means to consistently accomplish this, even as the business environment shifts. It also means dampening the impact that rolling out new products and services traditionally has on internal operations and suppliers. And it means doing the opposite from traditionally managed firms that insist on dumping their own burdens on the customer. Instead, it involves creating the means to protect customers from some of the turmoil that affects them as a result of difficult times.

A powerful result is the extraordinary degree of customer trust this creates—a deep recognition that these firms will continue to deliver the kinds of solid value that customers really need. Customers at Walmart, for instance, trust that they do not have to shop around to get a better price when they find an item they like. And travelers trust Southwest Airlines to offer the lowest fares and get them to their destinations on time—without the frustration of the hidden fees or reduced services demanded by its major competitors.

This very different focus leads to increased competitiveness even during challenging business conditions—often while others struggle to simply remain viable.

Mitigating Lag Versus Chasing the Problem

Business improvement efforts tend to focus heavily on problem solving—isolating specific areas where issues are most evident and then targeting them for action. Many of today's lean initiatives begin with an initial exercise to identify waste in organizations' value streams: finding excesses within the progression of activities required to transform their products or services from their most basic elements and deliver them to the customer. Once they identify excess inventories, processing steps, excessive transportation distances, or anything else that draws resources but does not directly add value to the customer, the typical natural inclination is to target these directly. Yet, too often the result is far less than what they expected.

While there is little doubt that mapping the value stream is an important step toward understanding the problems inherent in traditional management methods, it also creates a dangerous temptation for directly chasing these problems. The simple truth is that *the best solutions do not necessarily follow the problem.*

For instance, many begin at the end of the line, taking action where disruption accumulates and waste is most evident. But the underlying causes are often complex; correcting it might require making changes that are for less localized (as described in chapter 4). Moreover, what happens when "upstream" activities send disruption down the line to these "leaned out" operations? Disruption reemerges—probably even greater than before—overwhelming activities that no longer have buffers to dampen its effects.

What then should be the focus? Creating a structured solution that addresses the underlying reasons why waste accumulates in the first place. Rather than attempting to advance by using methods founded on the presumption that business will remain stable and predictable over time, those seeking to become lean must fundamentally rebuild their business to address the forces of uncertainty and change head-on.

This means successively addressing the lag that impacts each of the four elements involved in flowing value described earlier, implementing changes in a way that mitigates the dynamic effects that cause waste to accumulate, as will be described in subsequent chapters of this book. The result is farther-reaching benefits that organizations can much more quickly and consistently achieve.

Key Point: Why Chasing the Problems Is Not the Answer

Going Lean described that lean dynamics benchmarks like Toyota, Walmart, and Southwest Airlines did not attain their powerful capabilities by charging straight ahead at visible problems or implementing those initiatives that are most visible on the surface. Instead, they focused on transformational objectives for creating the underlying foundation of smooth flow on which their success depends (described in Chapter 6). Some important considerations for applying this focus include:

■ **Understand why changes are needed.** Because making changes to processes can be expensive and disruptive, understanding the bottom-line rationale and larger benefit is critical *prior* to embarking on waste reduction, standardization, or other process streamlining activities.

■ **Focus on *transformation* rather than following the problems.** To avoid targeting waste reduction without a central focus, a few simple questions should be considered: Are proposed efforts simply a way of stretching the current approach to doing business a little further? Is this the right sequence for these activities (per the framework described in Chapter 6)? Is this the best way for the business to spend its time, attention, and resources?

■ **Insist on *dynamic* transformation.** Rather than simply optimizing for steady-state conditions, efforts should focus on identifying and addressing disconnects in flow and the lag they create. This can help ensure that dynamic effects that create disruption and loss are being reduced.

■ **Relate *all* lean efforts to bottom-line metrics.** Too often programs aimed at discrete waste reductions do not take into account the great costs of generating them or the inadvertent shell game in which some areas gain at the expense of others (further explained in Chapter 6).

Promoting Dynamic Stability

How can corporations and institutions consistently meet or exceed customers' demand for dynamic value amid the challenging circumstances facing businesses today? Create a fundamentally different structure—one that is *dynamically stable*—that diminishes disruption to operations, decision making, information, and innovation in the face of changes or disruptions.

Traditionally managed companies tend to be dynamically unstable, meaning that they perform poorly when pressed to operate outside of their intended range of conditions. As described in *Going Lean*, the result is much like pushing a boulder up a hill: They must redirect enormous resources just to keep from falling backward. Firms demonstrating lean dynamics instead create a structure that accommodates a much broader range of circumstances, essentially flattening the hill—dampening variation before it has a chance to build. This lets workers and managers maintain their focus despite enormous shifts, rather than fall backward, as they otherwise might, with every new challenge.

How is this possible? Toyota, for instance, does this by deliberately mixing together and varying the types and quantities of items it makes on a given production line—producing each in small lot sizes that more closely approximate the rate of customer demand. This dramatically reduces demand uncertainty (which is instead amplified by traditional methods). Toyota's approach of co-producing *families of items* (groupings of items that share common characteristics so it is possible to seamlessly shift from processing one to the next) creates a mechanism for dampening the variation that changing conditions promote (an effect described in Chapter 4).

The result is creating the ability to dampen out the variation that traditionally results from sudden shifts, instead promoting the ability to sustain a consistent focus even during some of the most challenging circumstances. This helps these companies not only survive the downturns, but continue to advance innovation and pursue opportunities to create new value.

Challenging the "Culture of Workarounds"

American corporations and institutions are tremendously adept at dealing with crises. Their ability to overcome adversity and respond quickly when conditions do not turn out as planned has become essential to traditional business management methods. Rising to the top requires a strong capacity to make last-minute saves, like a football player who makes a diving catch in the end zone, for results that are immediate and visible. Yet such a culture runs counter to creating the consistent, dynamic value that is so critical to competing today.

Those striving to go lean must seek to create far greater consistency in their activities, designing their progression of work such that it can remain stable across the entire range of circumstances in which they operate. Lean capabilities, rather than individual heroics, mitigates the need for quick fixes; this can drive the capacity to sustain the rigorous and responsive progression of work, decision making, information, and innovation without the need for resorting to unplanned work, extra steps, or other wasteful measures in response to changing conditions. Achieving such consistency, however, takes more than restructuring the mechanical aspects of a business; it requires shifting the underlying culture that drives workarounds to flourish.

Changing this imbedded culture represents a central challenge for those implementing lean dynamics. People across the enterprise—managers, workers, and even suppliers—must understand that the most important part of the job is no longer last-minute heroics; instead, they must focus on preventing crises from occurring in the first place. Together personnel must create approaches for continuously improving the dynamic stability of the company and identify ways to forge ahead with new forms of value for the customer and corporation—regardless of the challenging conditions they might face.

Recognizing the Need for Transformation

Jack Welch observed that "only satisfied customers can give people job security. Not companies."[11] Nowhere is this clearer today than in America's automobile industry. For decades, its workforce and management focused on mitigating internal risks, seeking concessions that would strengthen their respective objectives for workforce protections and controlling labor costs. But all the while they missed the much greater risk—that building agreements based on past measures of success would only further entrench a way of doing business that was poorly suited to meeting the changing needs of their customers.

And now each side risks losing it all.

Firms and institutions must come to see that the real risk lies not in departing from what has become familiar but in sticking with what worked in the past. They must accept that the world is a much different place than it was when their traditional way of doing business was first created. Uncertainty and change have become the norm; customers today expect much more, and in the age of global business and the Internet, they have the means to get it. Conditions have become much more severe; case after case demonstrates the perils of standing still when challenges continue to evolve.

Despite its challenges, sustained excellence in this more severe business environment *is* possible—but only for those who are willing to step away from their false sense of security and embrace the principles that distinguish lean dynamics.

The critical challenge for most firms is not only to overcome their preconceived notions and recognize what going lean is really all about but also to translate it, beyond principles, into rapid, visible results and practices that address the real issues and challenges they face. Unfortunately, this is where lean efforts very often fall short. It is far easier to minimize meaningful principles in favor of slogans and simplistic plans that can be quickly grasped but do not build the needed foundation for sustained progress.

The next chapter describes some important steps to building a foundation and creating a case for a solid direction that will win deep-rooted support from everyone across the organization who will contribute. For this to succeed, however, each must clearly understand what must be done and why he or she must change in a way that is meaningful and actionable.

Key Point: Major Distinctions of a Lean Dynamics Approach

Lean dynamics recognizes that traditional methods designed for turning out value based on a presumption of stability and predictability have become stretched to their limits in today's environment of uncertainty and change. Value is dynamic; it is what customers say it is—even if they keep changing their minds. Lean dynamics is about adapting to this changing value and consistently driving efficiency, quality, and innovation across a wide range of conditions.

■ Traditional methods build in disconnects by design—gaps within operations, decision making, information, and innovation that together amplify variation and increase its disruptive effects. This *lag* typically goes unnoticed when forecasts prove steady and reliable. However, demand spikes or other sudden shifts ultimately lead to an exaggerated response when subjected to uncertainty and change.

■ The greater a business or an institution's lag, the greater the potential to overreact to changes, amplifying internal *variation* and increasing disruptive outcomes. This lag can come from a range of sources: from disconnects between measurement and outcome to discontinuous flow of information, operational steps, and decision making.

■ The best way to find lag is to identify its adverse outcomes, the most visible of which is the accumulation of *waste*. Waste is often the result of operating in dynamic conditions but with a management system optimized for stability.

■ The bottom-line result is a *loss* in value. Loss is the portion of the value that the business or institution must expend in order to turn out this value—including waste. Reducing waste is therefore critical to maximizing bottom-line value.

■ Going lean means more than addressing discrete elements of waste, each of which can have an uncertain impact on the bottom line. It means broadly minimizing loss—not only for existing circumstances but across the wide range of uncertain and changing conditions firms and institutions increasingly face as part of doing business within today's dynamic conditions.

The result is the strong, steady value—the ability to consistently innovate, profit, and advance into new markets within even the most severe conditions—that marks the benchmark of lean dynamics.

2 Creating a Sense of Excitement

IN 1999, Lion Brothers faced a serious challenge. Like many other firms, this leading manufacturer of apparel brand identification and decoration products had to find a way to correct the "Y2K" computer glitch that threatened to disrupt its information system with the coming of the New Year. As the company's leaders searched for a solution, they realized that far more could be done than applying the straightforward software upgrade that was originally envisioned. Bit by bit, they grew in their understanding of lean business practices—and realized that it was time to rethink their very way of doing business.

For much of its one hundred–year history, this family-owned business, headquartered in Baltimore, Maryland, had operated using a "piece-part" approach. Jobs were broken down by the various steps that went into turning out completed products—from cutting out the blanks, embroidering patterns, and stitching components together, to trimming and finishing. Supervisors issued tickets to track the number of units workers completed; the more they completed, the greater their compensation. The real challenge came from managing all of this, involving a primarily manual process of balancing units with steps completed at various stages of processing and tracking the compensation for those who had performed these steps—an administrative burden that no commercial software could readily accommodate.

Implementing a Y2K solution meant the company would have to fundamentally restructure to reduce its administrative complexity. This, however, would create a range of challenges, each of which was far from trivial. For one, management had to convince its unionized workforce that this change was not only important to the company but that it was in their own best interest.

The company's CEO, Susan Ganz, used this necessary change as the catalyst to set forth on an entirely different course. By creating outlets for its innovative capabilities, Lion Brothers could reach out in new directions, developing opportunities for growth in an industry in which others increasingly struggle to compete. But succeeding would require looking at the business in a very different way—transforming the way it operated, finding a means to better engage the customer, and building the flexibility to respond to continually shifting needs.[1]

Above all, it would mean gaining the understanding, participation, and even the excitement of not only its leaders but individuals across the workforce.

Setting a New Course

For Lion Brothers, identifying the challenge was fairly straightforward—the industry was rapidly moving overseas and losing business to low-cost producers—so it wasn't hard to see that things had to change. But which way should the company go? And how could it create the needed excitement to carry the company forward even when hard decisions had to be made—engaging the workforce and keeping it moving in this new direction over time?

The first step was to gain consensus among key stakeholders on which direction to turn. Those leading the effort needed to become fully convinced before beginning a journey they knew could shake up their operations. Managers needed to clarify for themselves how the end result would look; they had to build their own vision, plan for action, and case for change.

At the same time, people across the organization needed to develop a deep trust in this new direction. This was critical for reaching an agreement to shift from the popular piece-part mentality and to recognizing how individuals would personally benefit. Its lean efforts would need to engage people of all backgrounds and at nearly every level in a structured way, building an understanding that went deeper than slogans or management directives.

Bit by bit its leaders internalized the conviction that this was the right move, created the plan to achieve the shift, and began a dialogue that made it possible to convincingly guide their staffs as they encountered the challenges that came from the significant changes they would put in place.

Developing a New Philosophy

Going Lean describes the most basic step in moving forward as developing a *dynamic vision*. Too often companies and institutions lay out a path for improvement that represents little more than a continuation of what worked in the past—even when it should be clear that the business environment that once made success possible has fundamentally shifted.

Perhaps this is why developing a truly lean vision often requires outside help—if nothing else, consultants can more easily see past the current mindset that is so hard to break and make a cold, objective assessment about what makes sense and what must be changed. This requires some analytics—data-driven assessment that goes beyond the intuitive. Most of all, it requires a fundamental rethinking of what the business really seeks to accomplish and what will be necessary to achieve the new goals, based on a strong understanding of the different possibilities that result from going lean.

Lion Brothers stood out in that it recognized the need to rethink everything; its industry's fundamental shift had made it necessary to take a different approach altogether. Cost cutting alone could not be the answer; the company's Chinese factory already helped it meet the low-cost challenge and enabled it to compete in markets driven predominately by price. Yet it understood that continuing to thrive in the future would require much more. To better engage its customers, it needed to transform how it did business to create a more specific understanding of their needs. It needed to create methodologies that made it possible to quickly and flexibly deliver innovative products.

And it needed the ability to anticipate and provide for a broadening range of marketplace needs.

Meeting this challenge would demand a high degree of collaboration, new innovations to address emerging challenges and needs, and the means for quickly responding using flexible, cutting-edge operational capabilities. What it sought was to offer greater innovation, variety, and customized solutions than customers could get elsewhere. And so far the results seem impressive: Lion Brothers indicated that it continued to turn out significant profits in the face of growing overseas competition—even at the height of the 2008–2009 recession.

This focus—creating the means for better understanding the customers' increasingly complex and dynamic needs, coupled with dramatically more responsive internal capabilities that promote constant innovation and dynamic strategies—is what lean dynamics is all about. It means shifting from the presumption that all will remain stable to a way of thinking that more accurately projects that the environment and the customer will continually change.

Lion Brothers and others point to the importance of developing a clear view of what one's business will look like as the journey progresses. Executives, managers, and workers must understand the range of capabilities their company must possess to effectively respond to the dynamic challenges of its environment (which includes low costs—but goes much further). Leadership must learn to embrace a different ways of working, thinking, communicating, and innovating that together promote the creation of greater, cost-effective value—value that may not have been imagined before the transformation began (as described in Chapter 9).

Still, the most visible benefit of such an approach is that it forms a structure that progressively removes the greatest causes for waste to accumulate—thus creating rapid savings while preventing its recurrence as conditions continue to shift throughout its transformation. This is critical to sustaining trust that the shift is progressing as intended. But getting to this stage takes gaining the workforce's support in the first place; everyone across the business must come to embrace the philosophy and its underlying principles, which will point workers in the right direction.

Involving the Workforce

Organizations embarking on business improvement initiatives today seem to understand the importance of engaging the workforce—making their people central to the solution. However, many companies appear to do a poor job of making this work. A fundamental disconnect comes from how they introduce their way of doing business to the workforce—a problem that is often exacerbated by their implementation approach.

Many organizations begin their improvement initiatives by immediately organizing teams of workers to seek out and implement changes. This can create tremendous problems. As described in *Going Lean*, the division of labor that governs traditional management methods compartmentalizes work, decision making, and information in a way that limits individuals' "span of insight"—their ability to see the consequences of their actions. Immersing individuals in transformation activities before addressing this gap creates substantial problems—sometimes permanently alienating the workforce from the program and thwarting the possibilities for real improvement.

One common approach is to limit the scope of what they are asked to change—thus minimizing any disruption they might create. After completing some lean training, some workers are assigned to *kaizen* teams to identify improvements to an administrative function or some other activity peripheral to the business of the organization, whose disruption will not interfere with the broader activities of the business. Others might focus on actions aimed at increasing standardization or improving orderliness—applying "5S" methods as their primary emphasis as they seek to become lean.[2] Workers dive in and accomplish what they are asked—later recognizing that all of their efforts really did not make the meaningful difference to the business's competitiveness they hoped to achieve.

An alternate approach embraces the need to apply lean solutions to activities that strike at the core of a company's business. Teams are trained and charged with making real, substantial change. Despite their enthusiasm, their limited span of insight (a natural result of their functional divisions) can impact their focus; they can miss substantial implications that affect the vastly complex business, which they cannot be expected to fully understand. When briefed to top leaders who do have the span of insight, these gaps will likely be recognized—potentially causing staff recommendations to be abandoned.

This highlights a key dichotomy facing lean transformations: The workforce needs to be involved, yet the workforce's limited understanding restricts its central role in contributing to the solution. Proceeding without first addressing this natural disconnect can cause even well-intentioned actions to backfire, alienating workforces and undermining progress.

A critical first step is therefore creating a deliberate, structured approach for breaking down these barriers—beginning with making a sound, compelling case to spark everyone's interest and building a deep understanding of why this shift is in their own best interest. As discussed later in this chapter, this case for change must clearly describe to everyone—from top leadership to the entire workforce—where the business is going and why it is headed there. All must come to see that no other alternative exists; the only choices are to change or to perish—a perspective that their current way of doing business likely prevents many from seeing.

Making the Transformation Personal

The quality of a workforce's day-to-day actions must come from more than the company's lofty vision or even its specific objectives; those can point the way ahead but cannot by themselves inspire people to achieve excellence. How individuals will act is largely driven by the personal factors that they face—whether their jobs cause them to see the value they create and to interact with others around them.

Managers and workers must be given a specific focus and rationale that goes beyond the conceptual and makes the change specific and personal. This is consistent with what I found in my own career. I learned that people work best when their motivation comes from within; when they are empowered to take ownership themselves. They accomplish more when they are made accountable to each other—not simply to their boss. Once they and their peers more clearly understand their goals and why they are important, they themselves can take ownership to drive up team performance. The result can be far beyond anything that management directives could possibly achieve—most of all, ownership causes people to become happier at work.

A lean dynamics approach, therefore, begins by implementing a different construct that promotes more personal involvement. Jobs must be structured so that people can better understand how various job efforts support each other and realize the impact their work has on the customer, as well as on the company's bottom line. Workers should be measured for their accomplishments in promoting success against pertinent objectives instead of tracking efforts with unclear impact. Delegating decision making can increase agility and innovation; realigning information can promote simplicity while increasing the span of insight so necessary for eliminating lag.

Managers and workers must be given clear reasons why they are being asked to turn their world upside down and move in a direction that may not yet make sense—a graphic description of what is currently wrong and what direction the organization must take to correct it. Together all must come to see the crisis that surrounds them; they must understand how it is undermining their business or institution and threatening their combined interests. Moreover, they must come to understand that the solution is real—and attainable. Only then will they become capable of adapting to and adopting this construct for creating real, lasting value—and in doing so become more adept at protecting their real interests.

A great way to gain the necessary depth of insight might be through an offsite meeting to review the company or institution's stated vision, strategies, objectives, and metrics, both at the top level and within those parts of the organization where improvements have been most directly targeted. This can point to challenges and stimulate understanding of methods to address the growing reality of uncertainty and change.

Establishing a Dynamic Vision for the Future

The starting point of any lean journey must be to identify what "value" means within the specific context of the company's or institution's mission and to assess how well the organization is suited to deliver that value. A lean dynamics approach further recognizes that a fundamental tenet of creating value is directly responding to the customers' *dynamic needs*—giving them exactly what they want while sustaining the highest quality, lowest price, and greatest innovation, even when facing rapidly changing, unexpected circumstances.

How should an organization begin? By assessing its current state—determining how well the business as a whole is able to create value, not only for the conditions it anticipates but across the full range of dynamic circumstances it must face. A key focus should be its ability to create corporate value (e.g., profit, growth, or greater competitiveness) across dynamic conditions—something that is often not well understood.

Sustaining strong internal capabilities is a critical measure of a company's ability to create strong customer value, even in a crisis. Why is this? Think about a passenger jet's procedures in case of an emergency landing: Rather than placing the oxygen mask on your child, you are asked to first attend to yourself. The reason is simple: You must remain strong and capable in order to support those who depend on you. In much the same way, a company that prepares itself to avoid internal disruptions will be able to seamlessly continue to support its customers—preventing workarounds and waste that can undermine quality, consistency, and innovation.

A *dynamic value assessment* focuses on the business's value in response to dynamic conditions as a powerful means for understanding how well it is positioned to continue to serve its customers. It evaluates what the firm or institution produces today, how well it accomplishes this, and how well this meets its customers' needs. This includes an assessment of the dynamic conditions outside of the business—shifts in customer needs and desires, business conditions, and emerging opportunities and threats within its operating environment. From this, a rigorous evaluation of how well the organization will perform when it faces these conditions is conducted. (See Appendix A for a dynamic value assessment framework.)

This dynamic look at the business drives a different starting point from many of today's lean initiatives. Rather than correcting waste as it is found, it starts by looking across the business, from the company's suppliers to its customers. And instead of focusing where problems become most evident—at the end of the line such as a manufacturer's assembly operations—it seeks to identify the greatest sources of lag anywhere across its continuum of value creation that causes this waste to accumulate in the first place.

Starting with this dynamic value assessment is critical because it builds a baseline understanding of how well the company is structured to sustain value over time, progressively advancing the company's ability to create value in a way that makes it less likely to stumble despite the challenging circumstances it might face along the way.

Mapping the Value Curve

How is dynamic value measured? By using the *value curve*—a graphic representation of the organization's ability to generate bottom-line, tangible value as it responds to the broad range of dynamic conditions it must face. Figure 2-1 illustrates the value curve for a classic American corporation during a historic timeframe: General Motors

Figure 2-1. The Value Curve[3]

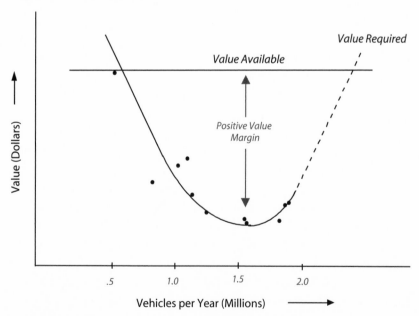

between 1926 and 1936, a string of years that swung from prosperity to the Great Depression.

What does this figure show us? It compares the company's value as perceived by its customers, assessed in tangible terms by what they are willing to pay for what the company produces (the top line in the figure representing the *value available* to the company) with the portion of this value necessary to produce these products (its *value required*). These are graphically compared to illustrate what is most important: their relationship across the company's range of business conditions (Appendix B describes the construction of the value curve).

We can see from its value curve that this example of a classic American corporation was not built for the dramatic shift in operating conditions it was forced to deal with. Like most traditionally managed corporations, it was designed to function efficiently within a narrower, specific rate of anticipated demand. The company's *value margin*—the portion of value that remains available to the corporation to maneuver—dropped off quickly as conditions significantly changed, a phenomenon marked by its steep, U-shaped curve.

Many companies today are governed by even steeper U-shaped value curves—a surprising development given decades of cost-improvement initiatives (it is how they apply such initiatives that seems to contribute to this result). Lean businesses, however, display a distinctly different focus, resulting in a dramatically different value curve pattern. Rather than optimizing for a narrow range of conditions, these firms perform consistently even when market conditions substantially change. As a result, they take in more value and expend less to do so, as is evident from the stark difference in their value curves.

Figure 2-2 illustrates the value curve for one such corporation, Southwest Airlines (depicted on the left of the chart), and compares its performance with one of its peers during the particularly challenging timeframe including the aftermath of September 11, 2001. Southwest's value curve looks virtually flat, a stark contrast to its competitor's steep, U-shaped curve. What does this tell us? The company continued creating steady value during the most difficult period this

Figure 2-2. Southwest Versus the Airline Industry[4]

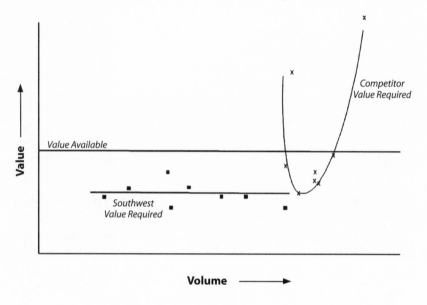

industry faced, while its peers struggled or fell into bankruptcy. It continued to offer sustained value as others grounded airplanes, abandoned gates, and furloughed employees. And it subsequently found opportunities to advance, expanding routes and picking up gates abandoned by competitors.

The value curve assessment offers a specific, objective means for raising awareness of the need to change directions. Its findings can point to a much more powerful program for improvement, not just for trimming costs, but for promoting dynamic strategies and responsive capabilities that are critical for sustaining bottom-line value. Moreover, they can serve as a valuable tool for gaining the buy-in across the workforce that is so critical yet so often absent.

By helping individuals understand the importance of change to the future of the corporation and building metrics that support the increments of change that they can better see are needed, people across the business can better understand why and how they must participate.

Key Point: How Do I Map a Value Curve?

An analyst sought to create a value curve for a business. After a couple of false starts, he quickly became proficient when he realized the process involved only five basic steps (additional details are provided in Appendix B).

1. **Measure the company's creation of *value*.** The analyst knew that the first step was to determine the company's *value available*—in tangible terms, what dollars were available for conducting all aspects of business. Upon reflection, he realized that this is the same as what customers perceive to be the value of the company's product: how much they are willing to pay for what the company offers, accounting for the other choices available and their changing needs, desires, and constraints over time (derived from the business's net sales).

2. **Relate this to what it takes to create this value.** He recognized that the company's *value required*—what it costs to create this value—is far from constant; it varies depending on the conditions that exist at the time. Rather than adding up the individual costs of all of its activities, expenditures, and wastes, he calculated this using a simpler, equivalent method: based on determining the difference between net sales and net income—a top-down way to determine costs within those conditions.

3. **Track the organization's response to changing demands.** Until this point, he could see nothing particular revealing; he needed to plot these results against a measure that would show how these related to each other across the company's entire range of operating conditions. This meant comparing the value available and value required for the number of products sold per year. (Note: this varies by business type, as described in Appendix B.)

4. **Plot the data.** To make the relationship between value available and value required more visible, he represented

value available as a constant and calculated and displayed its proportionally adjusted value required (Appendix B). He plotted the proportionally adjusted value available and value required points against the rate of demand each year over a ten-year timeframe.

5. **Evaluate the results.** The analyst found that the "curve" was optimal for only a narrow range of conditions, indicating that this company's lean efforts had not yet attained a result consistent with that seen for those at the highest level of lean dynamics, so he decided to investigate further (described in Appendix B).

Assessing the Challenges

By now the underlying focus in shifting to lean dynamics should be clear: to flatten the value curve—shifting from a steep V-shape to a less steep U-shape and ultimately to remain flat across a wide range of circumstances. Still, the value curve represents only a bottom-line indication of firms' maturity in attaining this goal. Advancing requires establishing and implementing a dynamic vision of the future consistent with those benchmarks that have pointed the way by attaining a flat value curve. The value curve breaks down our understanding of what they do into three basic components.

1. Creating and sustaining strong and sustainable *customer value*, translating to consistent *value available* to the corporation (the top line of the value curve) even in times of sudden demand shifts and changing needs

2. Building flexible, innovative, low-cost *internal capabilities*— or steady *value required* (flattening the U-shaped curve)— which are instrumental to supporting new opportunities that arise during challenging conditions

3. Establishing *dynamic business strategies* that flexibly respond to challenging conditions and promote a strong, steady *value margin* for continued value creation and advancement

Building a clear and compelling vision is critical. Doing so means formatting the specific challenges highlighted by the dynamic value assessment in a way that is easily understood by everyone across the business: corporate executives, stakeholders, suppliers, and individuals across the workforce (and perhaps even key customers). Using clear examples—presenting familiar problems and challenges within a context of today's dynamic challenges that will likely be brand new—this case must clearly show that there is no other choice but to make a change to lean dynamics.

In some cases, the threats might be particularly serious; companies might find themselves in a situation where the worst of the environmental dynamics described earlier have already struck. Firms' natural inclination is to react, as was described in the previous chapter. Clearly the first step is to regain stability; interim buffers, workarounds, or other wastes might be needed. By applying these as deliberate actions with the end goal in mind, they can help minimize any additional lag, while promoting the rigor, discipline, and span of insight needed to advance once operations stabilize.

Moreover, it is not enough to simply identify *that* the business or institution must change; determining its path to improvement is equally critical. Those leading the way must progressively mitigate the dynamic effects on their business and their customers, while pursuing different approaches to creating new forms of value, a key to thriving in today's competitive marketplace. It is therefore critical to identify a way that will lead to a fundamental shift in the value curve—something that will take time to achieve but, as this book will show, will create interim benefits that will help improve value and sustain the course as it progresses.

Key Point: Interpreting the Value Curve

The shape of the value curve offers powerful insights into an organization's underlying "leanness"—showing whether it is structured to meet the challenges it will increasingly face within today's increasingly dynamic environment. A steep, narrow, U-shaped value curve indicates that its way of doing business is optimized for stability and predictability, indicating that:

- **Inflexibility is inherent.** Companies that structure operations, decision making, information, and innovation to progress efficiently and effectively within only a narrow range of anticipated conditions are ill-suited to the challenges that occur when uncertain or changing conditions emerge. The result: *Loss skyrockets when conditions inevitably shift.*

- **Waste is built in as a fundamental way of doing business.** Traditional methods based on maximizing economies of scale inherently build in lag, which amplifies internal variation and disruption when subjected to change. Since waste is a natural response to this lag, the solution must be to address lag—not its outcomes—in order to mitigate this spiral of loss.

- **The solution must go beyond narrow targets.** *Going Lean* showed that firms can apply business improvement methods to save hundreds of millions of dollars without making a meaningful impact on the shape of their value curve. While cost cutting might be part of the answer, higher efficiencies across a broad range of conditions—the real need today—come from a fundamental restructuring rather than from simply attacking "waste."

- **Lean initiatives should not be peripheral to the central value-creation focus of the business.** What good does "leaning" a process do if its transformation has no impact on the value curve? The value curve's bottom-line measurement can help guide improvement activities toward staying on target, focusing them on what is really important to the company and its customers.

- **Customer needs must be well understood.** A steep value curve offers solid evidence that the company or institution does not fully understand its customers' dynamic needs. Perhaps it addresses them in aggregate, as if they all behave the same, or focuses on only limited portions of their needs. This can translate to poor responsiveness to real conditions, undermining customer trust and loyalty.

■ **A lean shift will take time.** Although implementing lean dynamics can produce rapid, dramatic benefits, shifting from a steep U-shape to the advanced state marked by a flat value curve will not occur overnight. Still, the value curve can serve as a reliable beacon on the horizon, guiding the way. In conjunction with intermediate measurements it can show progress along a pathway that may otherwise create confusion.

CHAPTER

3 The Road to Lean Advancement

G OING LEAN BEGAN with a simple observation: "Excellence is best seen in a crisis." The way in which a business responds when confronted with a major challenge points to its deeper capabilities, not only for avoiding the dramatic breakdowns so widely seen today, but for reaching forward to embrace fresh opportunities and set new value standards as business conditions continue to evolve.

The value curve is particularly powerful because it clearly depicts this phenomenon by graphically illustrating firms' bottom-line capabilities for sustaining steady value across the breadth of conditions they might face. Those demonstrating greater preparedness and adaptability within today's dynamic conditions often advance to lead their industries in key measures of performance (demonstrated in *Going Lean*), reinforcing the value curve as the new yardstick for measuring a business's progress.

Yet attaining value curve excellence is a significant and challenging undertaking. Companies do not transform themselves to a flat curve in a single leap; rather, the evidence points to a need for a carefully structured program that progressively mitigates major sources of lag and loss over a number of years on the journey toward this state of sustainable excellence. Staying on course, therefore, requires tracking one's progress against a beacon on the horizon (such as the promise of attaining a flat value curve).

Complicating matters is the reality that such projects rarely begin from scratch—most are affected by either progress or false starts from previous efforts. Some organizations might have realized initial successes with lean tools or practices; still others might have stumbled, leading personnel across the business to simply increase their resistance to change. Either way, firms must begin by reassessing where they stand and where they are going, maximizing what lessons they have learned and capabilities that already exist, and setting a course for overcoming the hurdles that stand in their way.

Beginning the Journey

Like many aerospace producers, Cessna Aircraft Company began experimenting years ago with techniques to improve the efficiency of its operations. It began by applying lean and Six Sigma tools as tactical fixes—"planting seeds" for improvement across a wide range of activities, from operations to finance and legal support, whose bottom-line benefits were only generally understood.[1]

This methodology is not much different from what is commonly applied within companies and institutions of all types today. Many seem to focus on eliminating wastes, identifying areas where extra inventories, padded schedules, and extra processing steps are clearly evident and then "leaning" them out. Often this begins with work standardization or other efforts aimed at tightening existing business activities to make businesses operate more smoothly while minimizing operational costs—quickly and visibly generating savings before declaring victory and moving on to another project.

What makes Cessna's efforts stand out is the deeper understanding that seems to have sprouted from widespread experimentation. It increasingly shifted focus from fostering localized wins to attaining deeper transformation. While the company continues to encounter significant bumps in the road, its fundamental shifts in philosophy, changes in organizational structure, and more substantial implementation methods seem to have kept it on course, improving the dynamic stability of its operations while progressively transforming the business as a whole.² The way in which it moved beyond its initial stages and its determination to press forward through difficult times offer important insights into the road to lean maturity.

Seeing Beyond Traditional Solutions

As is often the case, Cessna's greatest advancement grew out of crisis. It stemmed from a need to overcome a major challenge when demand for its airplanes suddenly spiked to several times beyond normal levels. The result was immediate and dramatic; what worked well when production was at 75 jets per year no longer sufficed when production quickly grew to between 300 and 400 planes. Parts shortages skyrocketed; schedule interruptions broadly impacted the progression of work.

The company quickly recognized that slashing waste was not in itself the answer; waste reduction would do little to overcome the dynamic challenges it faced. What it really needed was a means for improving predictability within its operations despite extreme change and unpredictability, preventing loss from skyrocketing while increasing its available capacity.

> Our focus shifted to things like ramping up production to accommodate 10 more jets, or to slashing service time to keep our customers' aircraft in the air—not cost, which became more of a strong secondary consideration. We began asking ourselves why we are doing this, instead of how.
>
> Tim Williams, Cessna's VP for Lean Six Sigma³

Cessna's challenge was not unique; it illustrated a condition that has long plagued the business of aerospace: companies' struggle against operational turmoil arising from sudden spikes and downturns in customer needs, translating to difficulty in signaling and coordinating activities across its vast, complex string of activities. Parts shortages are not uncommon; production delays, "traveled work" (completing work steps at subsequent stations to keep from holding up later steps), and other workarounds are normal steps that seem widely accepted as the way things work. Consider the challenge described decades ago:

The problem of scheduling aircraft fabrication is what one might call "complicated simplicity." It is not all academic or a series of numbers that can be multiplied and divided to get the answer. Much of the success of any scheduling system is due to the use of plain "horse sense" by the scheduling personnel.

Production manager for Beech Aircraft, 1943[4]

Like many firms across this industry, Cessna had become accustomed to the internal turmoil that comes from such shifts. However, the understanding it had gained from its lean "Black Belt" efforts seemed to spark a deeper recognition that real change was possible. The company's focus began to shift. Less and less attention was given to the dollar savings of these efforts; attention shifted to understanding the real, bottom-line impact of these activities on overcoming its deeper issues. What was once a series of niche projects became increasingly understood for their deeper importance, with their contributions increasingly linked to and reported against the corporation's strategic plan and objectives.

Finding the Road to Lean Maturity

Cessna knew that it needed greater flexibility to respond to suddenly shifting demands and cancelled orders, continual production and configuration shifts, and changing delivery sequences and shifting customer requirements. This shift in thinking toward identifying clear focal points for its transformation (a concept described in Chapter 6) fostered a fundamental change from applying lean and Six Sigma tools for moving in a general direction toward concentrating on meaningful but manageable elements and addressing them through a structured progression of activities.

It became clear that chasing the problems where they became most evident was not the answer; the root cause for disruptions in assembly could often be traced far upstream, often to problems within its supplier base. Part of the problem was the complexity of Cessna's sourcing approach, which depended on a vast supplier base whose layout was far from intuitive. Multiple suppliers provided the same types of parts, fragmenting demand and amplifying uncertainty.

Moreover, the company's work with its suppliers had revealed a number of challenges the company was creating itself.

This realization sparked a focus on fundamentally transforming how the company structured and managed its supplier base. One element was its Center of Excellence (COE) program, a series of efforts focused on optimizing its supply base by narrowing it down to include only "very select suppliers based on their dedicated support to product families" (an important concept further described in Chapter 4).⁵ The company leverages its cross-functional commodity team to scrutinize the details of thousands of parts and components, identifying commonalities in materials, processing characteristics, or other features that point to synergies that would enhance suppliers' ability to become more efficient and quickly respond to changing needs. By choosing suppliers based on their ability to create efficiencies by producing parts for specific product families and procuring items based on their alignment to these families, the team has slashed its costs and dramatically reduced lead times.

The company's supplier efforts over the last decade have led to powerful results: Suppliers' on-time deliveries improved from 42 percent up to 99 percent, and their quality defects dropped from a high of over 11,000 per million to 550 as of the end of 2008, while achieving substantial cost reductions. But the impact on the core focus for change—reducing disruption due to problems with material availability—is particularly impressive. Stock-outs for the 74,000 part numbers delivered plummeted from over 1,000 per week at its peak to an average of only 6 per week in 2008.⁶

Cessna's increasing lean maturity is evident in its evolving organizational structure. The company previously aligned its substantial pool of Black Belts—set at 1 percent of its total workforce—under a central office, shared with operational units as needed to provide insight and support to their efforts. Their accomplishments were measured in the same piecemeal way, estimating savings from individual lean projects. At the end of 2008, this all changed. The company now places its Black Belts directly into the organizational elements they support—a structure that normally would have brought tremendous risk that individuals would simply be redirected to performing day-to-day work. But so far, this has not been the case; improvement efforts do not seem to be dropping off. With this, Cessna had made a leap in lean maturity—it progressed from implementing lean as a series of discrete, separately managed projects to an accepted, central part of managing the business.[7]

These results are particularly powerful in that they demonstrate that lean methods can extend beyond the simpler environments that most often serve as examples; it shows that powerful gains are possible within one of the most complex business environments—offering potential that extends well beyond aerospace. Hospitals, for instance, might face uncertain demand, treating patients who have widely ranging backgrounds and needs—yet managed using a system designed for sameness and stability. Educators face an enormous challenge; they operate within a structure built for tremendous stability, while they increasingly face the need to constantly and quickly respond to market changes and the individualized needs of their customers—a dramatic shift from the stable, standardized course offerings and delivery methods under which these institutions thrived in the past.[8]

Each of these faces a common challenge: They need to overcome the temptation to follow the path that so many others are taking and instead transform to better operate within an environment that is very different from what they faced in the past. Most importantly, they must recognize that this transformation does not come in a single step; improvement occurs incrementally. It takes progressive growth in understanding, capabilities, and breadth of application over time to advance lean maturity in a steady and structured way.

The Five Levels of Lean Maturity

Too often I hear lean practitioners declare that going lean can be boiled down to a single term: "continuous improvement." Unfortunately, this sets the bar very low—it offers a great excuse for approaching lean in any way or fashion a manager might choose. Within that context, almost any gains at all can be considered a success. After all, can anything be considered a failure if lessons are learned from mistakes along the way?

Continuous improvement (or *kaizen*, in lean terminology) is clearly a central part of any program for going lean, just as are the many tools and practices that make up a lean methodology. Yet managers should not simply apply lean tools in an intuitive manner. Applying lean tools and practices without first establishing a corporate-wide, end-to-end overarching structure might serve only to refine the status quo—reinforcing the way their company or institution already operates, within the plateau at which it already exists.

This is perhaps the greatest challenge for corporations and institutions: seeing past their current performance level and recognizing the means—and the need—to move to a different level altogether. This is particularly evident from looking at lean efforts today; firms and institutions seem to plateau at distinct levels of maturity. Why does this happen? Perhaps because firms and institutions become satisfied with continuous improvement *within* these plateaus. By applying tools and practices aimed at stretching what worked well a little further they make incremental improvements that yield quick victories rather than long-term advancements in corporate competitiveness and value.

The problem this creates for companies and institutions should be clear to readers by now; real success within today's dynamic environment takes breaking out of their current mold to shift upward to an entirely new level of performance. But doing so requires seeing past the traditional view of continuous improvement, instead aiming their efforts toward advancing to higher levels of maturity. Finding the way to accomplish this means putting together the lessons from today's vast experimentation—the principles, experiences, and skills proven over time to advance firms or institutions to the next level—and finding the means for navigating through the natural sticking points in the progression toward achieving sustainable value.

Recognizing the Plateaus

Companies generally appear to begin their journeys much as was done at Cessna: as a series of projects, tackling discrete issues in a tactical manner. But Cessna was able to advance beyond this; it saw the need to pursue higher levels of maturity. What are these levels? After observing and researching lean initiatives over time, I began to see a pattern. Despite focusing on "continuous improvement," all lean efforts do not appear to continuously progress. Instead, they appear to fall into a series of plateaus—distinct levels of their advancement in maturity, as depicted in Figure 3-1.

Figure 3-1. Levels of Lean Maturity

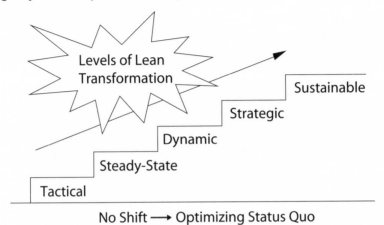

The most basic level is no shift at all—simply accepting the status quo, tightening up existing processes using a wide range of measures aimed at better dealing with the challenges firms or institutions face today. Many seem intent on applying modern tools and techniques, ranging from information technology solutions to long-term supplier arrangements, as a means to overcome the disconnects that cause increased costs that impact their bottom lines. Yet, while these appear to succeed in cutting costs, they might also create increased inflexibility to change—amplifying the downward spiral of loss when later subjected to uncertainty and change.

A much more common starting point is implementing *tactical lean*—an array of initiatives driven by the general rhetoric of "cutting the fat." Many companies and institutions today fall into this category; they tend to attribute virtually any savings to "lean"—presumably as a means for demonstrating their success to senior management. Without sufficient attention to deeper, more transformational activities, efforts can stagnate after an initial increment of improvement, causing a serious loss of support if workers and managers see it as a superficial fix rather than a means for addressing the more serious challenges that remain. In some cases this first step could be portrayed as a *step down*. It can create barriers to lean improvement that far exceed the first-level savings realized from pockets of waste reduction.

More advanced is *steady-state lean*—an end-to-end approach to addressing issues affecting the operational flow of a value stream. These efforts often begin in pursuit of whatever challenge presents itself first, with a primary emphasis on eliminating waste within current operating conditions. Some businesses progress farther, advancing to apply many of these principles to attain an increased focus on *dynamic lean*—leveraging lean tools and practices to create an ability to right themselves when things go wrong, maintaining internal stability and, therefore, more consistent delivery of value, despite uncertain or shifting conditions (these levels are discussed further in Chapter 7).

Companies like Toyota go farther still, advancing to *strategic lean*—pursuing new business strategies by drawing on their greater internal stability to create steady, growing value across a broad range of circumstances. Companies like Southwest Airlines appear to have advanced to the ultimate maturity level—attaining what might be described as *sustainable lean*. These businesses have succeeded in so deeply entrenching the principles of lean dynamics that their value curves—the hallmark of lean—remain virtually flat even in today's crisis. They look beyond such traditional measures as market share and advancing at a strong but cautious pace. Perhaps more importantly, they succeed in driving a fundamental shift in how leaders view the creation of value for their customers—reaching out to transform the business environment and reshape customer expectations to better value their capabilities.

Their sustained excellence demonstrates what some have long surmised—that restructuring to a different way of doing business can overcome many of the challenges that have been traditionally simply accepted as part of doing business. These organizations ultimately transform the business environment itself—raising the bar for value across the industry and transforming expectations for customers and the workforce alike.

Creating a Structure for Advancement

What is particularly important about recognizing these levels of lean maturity is the visibility it can create for companies regarding the range and challenges of lean projects. By understanding the continuum of this journey, those leading the efforts can better understand where they stand now and where they must go from there.

Businesses that plateau at one of these levels can run into a number of critical challenges. For instance, they might lose the support of their workforce when personnel tire of stagnating well below the potential gains touted by those leading the efforts (as well as top managers who wish to shift to other initiatives that hold greater promise). Moreover, they might encounter environmental turmoil that undermines the progress of efforts that have not reached sufficient maturity to sustain results (described in Chapter 4). Either of these can cause initial gains to erode; perhaps more damaging is the risk of undermining the workforce's belief in lean as a meaningful solution.

Thus, simply embarking on a program of unstructured continuous improvement is not enough. By instead working toward stabilizing their positions while striving toward the next levels of maturity, it stands to reason that they will increasingly reduce the potential that disruptive forces can lead to backsliding or abandoning their efforts altogether.

Key Point: Assessing Your Starting Point

An important first step is to identify where on the continuum of lean maturity one's organization stands. This can help point to the general mindset that exists—a key foundation for creating the vision, case for change, and plan of action that can set the course to advancing to sustainable lean (the ultimate state of maturity represented by a flat value curve). This is a critical step; it is most important in the organization's potential to continue to advance despite the pressures to stagnate and simply refine gains within a given level of maturity. Some questions that can help include:

■ Does your company or institution focus many initiatives on attaining different targets, such as faster inventory turns or cost reductions? Are tool descriptions, such as 5S and value stream mapping, intertwined in these targets? If the answer is yes, it is probably firmly fixed on a tactical lean plateau.

■ Rather than accumulating discrete cases of waste reduction, do you instead seek to create a deeper capability for leveling flow from end to end across the enterprise? Have you identified clear objectives and metrics that readily tie to bottom-line results, driving workers and managers to emphasize this focus in their day-to-day duties? If so, your business might have reached the level of *steady-state lean*, realizing such broader benefits as freeing capacity to be applied toward other areas needing transformation.

■ Would you consider your business improvement methods to be focused on enhancing processes or on value as defined by the customers, even if they keep changing their minds? This is a critical distinction that points to a focus on *dynamic lean*. Emphasizing process redesign can cause leaders to become fixated on *how* to achieve an existing target, instead of exploring *what* that target should be. Seeking instead to understand the dynamics of value and focus on optimizing its incremental buildup can redirect attention to opportunities for transformation at each step along the way.

■ Do maximizing innovation and seeking new opportunities factor heavily into your approach to lean? Are product families optimized with this in mind; are design personnel, top executives, and other parts of the organization showing great interest and involvement in your progress and contributing as team members for identifying and rolling out new phases in your progression? If this is the case, you may be approaching or at the level of *strategic lean*.

■ Does your organization break from the tradition of fixating on attaining market share, instead focusing on ways to sustainably advance in creating customer and corporate value? Is your value curve flat? You may have attained the elite rank of *sustainable lean*, a level that only a limited number of organizations have reached. If this is the case, you already know that your journey is far from complete; retaining this capability takes constant vigilance, innovation, and hard work, but doing so creates enormous satisfaction, not only for the customer but for individuals across the organization as well.

PART

2 Structuring for Lean Dynamics

THE FUNDAMENTAL ASSUMPTIONS a company or an institution makes at the outset of a major project can have far greater impact than any of the work it subsequently performs. Why is this? Because the way in which its leaders see the challenge ultimately guides how they structure everything—from the scope of the project, to evaluating existing constraints, to determining what path they choose to achieve these objectives. Breaking through traditional presumptions and seeking real transformation are therefore critical to making a lean project succeed.

Chapter 4 describes how gaining a deep understanding of the challenge can fundamentally alter the way companies and institutions implement lean. By reaching beyond visible symptoms and applying methods to fundamentally shift the way value is constructed, they can quickly achieve much greater results from the same set of lean tools and practices.

Chapter 5 explores ways of breaking through traditional organizational barriers by restructuring individuals' responsibilities, the way they use information, and the manner in which they work together to create the insight, inclusion, action, and integration they need—a key element to implementing this shift.

Chapter 6 concludes this part by describing common hazards that cause lean initiatives to plateau and explores where to begin—describing how identifying focal points for transformation can structure improvement efforts around what is most important for the business, helping overcome the roadblocks that keep so many of today's efforts from advancing in maturity.

4 Building a New Foundation

IN 1903, mechanical engineer Frederick Winslow Taylor proposed a business philosophy that promised to unleash new levels of productivity. His principles of *scientific management* held that dividing workers' individual tasks into their smallest components, coupled with their strict standardization and control, would permit great advances in productivity. For decades, this clear division between the realms of performing work and its management served as the basis for business management, leading the way for unprecedented increases in productivity.[1]

Managers everywhere have come to realize the shortfalls of Taylor's principles, particularly in today's environment, in which workers' knowledge and broader participation have become more valued. A focus on managing work as a collection of isolated activities undermines workers' insight into the contribution of their efforts to bottom-line value; applying rigid top-down controls to regulate the details of day-to-day activities discourages individual creativity.

Still, today's business improvement methods can seem to drift down this same path.

It is not hard, for instance, to find consultants armed with process maps and sticky paper pads scrutinizing time and motion in a manner that, to the casual observer, can look much the same as that of Taylor's early efficiency experts—speeding work steps and moving activities closer together in order to shave precious seconds from production. Why do companies accept this? The short-term benefits can seem appealing. Companies and institutions have reported significant cost savings, a tantalizing prospect to those struggling with the challenges of today's economic downturn.

Consider the approach employed by Starbucks, perhaps the most recognizable name in high-end coffee retail. The company purportedly has sent its vice president for lean, along with a ten-person team, from region to region with a focus that seems simple and clear: Slash the time that workers spend in unproductive motion. The approach? Teach managers to overcome waste by challenging them to assemble and then break down a Mr. Potato Head toy in less than forty-five seconds.[2]

Yet, for a business that seeks to capture premium prices for distinctive, hand-crafted products, it is hard to understand how the apparent objective of trimming a couple of seconds of wait time—an improvement that few customers are likely to notice—is reason to declare success. And these methods seem to be alienating at least some within its workforce—the very people upon whom going lean most depends.[3]

Somehow the real goal seems to have been lost along the way. Going lean should mean far more than applying process improvement tools and techniques to stretch traditional methods a little farther; it should accomplish more than simply trimming a few seconds of time or cutting an increment of inventory. Instead, it should be about adopting an entirely different philosophy that fundamentally alters the way companies and institutions will do business. It should focus on identifying and restructuring the building blocks of value in a way that can drive real transformation and broadly advance against deeper challenges and, in doing so, quickly achieve much greater results from the same set of lean tools and practices.

But doing so requires taking a step back and challenging what appear to be common misunderstandings about implementing lean principles.

Seeing Beyond the Waste

One of the most recognizable activities organizations perform as they embark on going lean is creating a *value stream map*: a graphic that depicts the progression of information and activities involved in either producing or developing a product or service to meet customer demands. Its application in one form or another has grown so broadly that this tool is now widely regarded as being almost synonymous with going lean.

A classic example of the value stream map is the creation of a cola can, described by James Womack and Daniel Jones in *Lean Thinking*. The authors depict the sequence of all the activities that go into its production—from mining bauxite ore, through its transformation into aluminum sheets as it progresses through a mill, smelter, and a series of rollers; transportation to the can producer, bottler, store, and a number of warehouses along the way; until it finally reaches the customer's home. Tracing the can's step-by-step progression from its most basic elements to its final form and destination makes visible the substantial delays, extra effort, and other wastes that fall between actual processing steps. In total, the vast majority of time—more than 99 percent—is spent waiting, with its materials handled more than 30 times, stored and retrieved 14 times, palletized 4 times—with 24 percent of the material never making it to the customer.[4]

Because the value stream map looks at the creation of value in an entirely different way, it offers a striking view of how disconnected operations can be—and how riddled with waste they are by design. *Going Lean* describes the reason for this: The traditional emphasis on optimizing factories for turning out huge batches of identical items at a narrow, anticipated rate of demand drives the adoption of supersized equipment to create large economies of scale—and with it a focus on keeping people and equipment operating efficiently, without regard to the tremendous waste that comes with this.

The challenge, however, is determining what to do with this insight. Too often these value stream mapping exercises serve merely as a backdrop for simplified waste reduction exercises, in which teams assembled from the workforce are asked to tag waste, claiming quick "savings" by reducing excesses where they are seen. And these efforts often presume that waste is simply the result of sloppiness and poor oversight, rather than a symptom of the deeper disconnects described in this book.

In reality, recognizing waste is only a starting point—understanding *what drives this waste* is most critical and requires significantly more digging.

Learning to See Why

When I assess a factory, I generally begin by walking the floor, starting at final assembly and working my way backward. This lets me quickly get a sense of how lean the facility really is, since disruption and waste are most evident at the end of the line, where all of the problems come together. For many businesses, this is where the assessment ends; they quickly act on these findings, draw down waste, and then move on to the next project.

Such an approach, however, does not necessarily lead to the best results. For instance, one facility I visited recounted how its focus on waste reduction led it to slash its inventories by 20 to 30 percent. The results were severe—stock-outs and workarounds soon mounted to a point that nearly crippled its operations. What was the lesson? Although large inventories point to the existence of a problem, addressing only the symptoms is not the answer. The challenge companies face is not so much in understanding *that* something must be done but determining *what* must be done and how best to proceed.[5]

Where, then, should one begin? After identifying the existence of waste, an organization must dig much deeper to isolate the sources of lag that cause this waste to emerge. A great starting point is using a simple, yet powerful, lean technique known as the "5 Whys." Toyota found that repeatedly asking the question "Why?" creates a very different plane of understanding and ultimately leads companies or institutions to structuring deeper, more meaningful solutions.[6]

Each response to the question "Why?" develops a deeper understanding of the underlying challenges. The first answer might make the solution seem as easy as tightening up operating procedures and

standardizing work steps (which is where actions often seem to cul-
minate). By the end, however, the need for a more complex, entirely
different solution might become clear. Rather than focusing on intuitive answers such as shortening travel distances or eliminating
steps where waste is most visible, greater scrutiny shows that creating lasting, more meaningful solutions comes from looking farther
and deeper—toward upstream challenges, organizational and information disconnects, or other sources of lag that cause disruption to
accumulate.

Understanding that a problem exists is only the beginning; next
must come probing questions aimed at understanding *why* the problem exists.

Key Point: The Power of Asking "Why"

When seeking to understand the cause for high production costs
at a complex manufacturing facility, consider how asking the
question "Why?" five times can lead to a completely different
path to improvement than is revealed by the first response:

■ When walking the production line, suppose that you find
widespread indications of waste: extra work steps, out-
of-sequence activities, stockpiles of parts, and partially
constructed components that have not moved in a long
time. **Why?**

■ There may appear to be a number of contributing reasons,
but suppose most boil down to poorly synchronized activities that cause disruption at various stations in the production sequence. **Why?**

■ On the surface, these disruptions can seem to be the fault of
unreliable schedules. However, a deeper look might show
that many stem from problems with suppliers: late deliveries and high quality-rejection rates for critical parts. **Why?**

■ Perhaps answering this question reveals that suppliers
struggle to deliver these items when needed because they

are needed so infrequently, making demand difficult to forecast. Keeping in stock all items that could potentially be needed might be too expensive. And further scrutiny might show that producing them once demand arises takes months or even years (a challenge that is not uncommon in aerospace and defense, as in the case described at the end of this chapter). **Why?**

■ The problem could be that they contain expensive raw materials that have very long lead times; these can take months to produce after demand for the part materializes. **Why?**

■ Perhaps because its procurement team does not have the capability, training, or insight to structure contracts in a way that addresses supplier challenges that will impact the suppliers' business.

Demanding a Fundamental Shift

Advancing beyond tactical lean initiatives toward greater lean maturity requires asking questions that reach far beneath the surface in order to recognize the real challenges that drive waste accumulation. The answers to these questions can lead to a very different starting point. Rather than beginning by improving discrete processes or value streams, those leading the effort must first understand the broader reasons for the greatest problems they find—disconnects that drive overreaction, workarounds, and inefficiencies each time conditions shift.

Consider the example above. Asking "Why?" five times revealed entirely different challenges than might have been initially perceived. The extra work steps and inventories seen on the shop floor were a result of a deeper issue. Rather than remove them directly (which might have increased disruption), the real answer is to address a supplier base issue, perhaps by creating multidiscipline procurement teams better equipped to structure purchases in a way that can help suppliers deal with the sources of lag that undermine their performance (like Cessna did, as described in Chapter 3).

This illustrates an important challenge for lean activities everywhere. Those leading these efforts must shift focus from simply driving rapid savings to demanding the fundamental shifts that going lean is all about. They must come to expect more than quick gains from first-order waste reduction and become intent on identifying a new structure for building up value without the disconnects that create lag and loss along the way.

But where should one begin? Enhancing one process area at a time (often the recommended path for value stream progression) offers little relief to a factory where managers are dealing with widely ranging issues.7 Targeted problem-solving methods that intuitively point the way for simple products with fairly straightforward value streams give much less insight into how to proceed within businesses whose vast complexity and scope present myriad potential starting points.

Just as with other aspects of a lean solution, the answer comes down to understanding the end-to-end progression of activities—beginning by rethinking how businesses and institutions put together the building blocks for value.

Assessing the Foundation of Value Creation

We have seen throughout this book that going lean begins with seeing the gaps in the way work is currently managed—beginning at the end of the line where problems accumulate, and then working backward to better understand their causes. By mapping the sequence of processing steps for even a cola can, described earlier in this chapter, it becomes clear that creating value can follow a seriously disconnected pathway, filled with delays, wasteful efforts like repeated palleting and warehousing, and substantial material scrap along the way.

But how can one assess these disconnects across a much more expansive business—like so many today that produce complex products across vast operations? Lean practitioners typically fall back on mapping the value stream; unfortunately, using this method means truncating the map to include only a limited portion of the processing steps in order to maintain a workable scope.8 Yet, narrowly defining the stream of activities in this way can seriously limit the assessment; it stands to miss many important interactions that contribute to the lag that causes much of the waste their efforts seek to address.

Thus, while value stream mapping offers an important means for *seeing the problem*, applying it as an initial step for addressing the complex challenges many firms face presents severe limitations.9 Refined, localized processing sequences can miss broader issues that must first be addressed. Moreover, even the best improvements might represent only a tiny thread of excellence woven through a vast fabric of activities that remains riddled with disruption and loss. Benefits from improving truncated value streams might be swallowed up within such a complex system.

Firms and institutions can avoid this by conducting a broad assessment of the challenges and interactions throughout their business before launching into targeted improvement activities. The *dynamic value assessment* (described in Appendix A), offers a structured means to accomplish this. It focuses on gaining fundamental insights into how well operations respond to changing conditions—from shifts in customer needs and desires, to changes in business conditions, to the emerging opportunities and threats that many increasingly face. By systematically reviewing their overall effectiveness in responding to these circumstances, it offers the means to structure a comprehensive approach to progressively addressing the underlying issues—the sources of lag that can undermine their business results.

Beginning with this overarching look at the business will likely drive a different starting point than would otherwise be selected. For instance, rather than correcting waste where it is most apparent—at the end of the line, such as in a manufacturer's assembly operations where problems become most evident—firms can target those areas of greatest lag that cause this waste to accumulate in the first place, and thus create the greatest impact to bottom-line results.

An important outcome of this assessment, therefore, is identifying critical focus areas within a structure for moving forward based on the organization's current challenges and needs (described in Chapter 5). These *transformational focal points* can provide needed direction for structuring improvement projects, progressing from mitigating baseline disruption to aligning by *product families*—a critical enabler for creating dynamic stability. As we will see in Chapter 5, these focal points can serve as a means for structuring improvement initiatives to progressively extend individuals' insight and involvement—enabling them to take part in addressing major challenges. Their efforts can help in achieving everything from improving baseline stability, to reducing setup times and creating more dynamic supplier arrangements that are important to progressing in lean maturity.

In essence, the dynamic value assessment can serve as a bridge for applying tools and practices that tend to work well for simpler products within stable environments to vast businesses producing complex products or services subjected to dynamic operating conditions—essentially scaling them up so they can be applied in a manner for more consistent, powerful results.

Harnessing Product Families as a Foundation for Lean

Assessing how value is created is a fairly complex undertaking. It requires scrutinizing not just the end product but each of the many elements, or *increments of value,* that go into building it. For a complex product like a car or an airplane, there might be hundreds or thousands of these elements—each representing distinct increments of value that must be designed, produced, and delivered when needed by a customer. Deciding how these distinct elements will be managed is particularly critical because, in many ways, it sets the foundation for everything that follows.

But where is the best place to begin?

Manufacturers capture these increments of value using a *bill of materials* (BOM): a classification of all of the materials, parts, and components that go into their products and the parts that go into them. This serves as the basis for everything from how they plan and execute production, to planning capacity, to scheduling operations. In essence, the BOM represents a roadmap to creating value, showing the important contribution of each element within the final product—how each of these items that a company or its suppliers must optimally create align with other elements at any given point in production.

In my study of aerospace manufacturing, early attention to the BOM was a fundamental differentiator between businesses that substantially benefited from their lean efforts and those that did not.[10] While most had been able to reduce waste, those that had first established an accurate, detailed understanding of what went into the finished product (despite periodic design changes) demonstrated substantially greater bottom-line benefits.

What does this tell us? Before charging ahead to find opportunities for waste reduction, why not begin by refocusing attention on what it is these serve to produce—*the product itself*? After all, it is creating this value that is at the heart of lean; operational steps are simply the means to achieving this end. Reconsidering how production planners originally structured these elements (most likely as stand-alone elements to promote economies of scale under the presumption of stable, predictable demand) and shifting instead to a product family orientation wherever possible can create far more benefit than simply focusing on improving existing processes.

Why make this change? Shifting to manage by product families can create a far-reaching result that could potentially impact hundreds or even thousands of individual value streams that have yet to be mapped, creating solutions that otherwise might never have been possible.

Promoting Variation Leveling

Despite the importance of product families, many lean efforts appear to spend little time evaluating their makeup, instead quickly leaping ahead to the more tangible tasks of mapping the processing steps within their value streams. Product families are often identified as the *end items* that are delivered to the customer. For instance, a product family for an automobile producer might be a family of cars, a mindset that misses the opportunity to draw on commonalities across their increments of value. This focus significantly limits their ability to leverage one of product families' greatest benefits: a structure for promoting *variation leveling*—dampening out internal disruption that is caused by shifts in the environment.

Figure 4-1 illustrates the mechanism for creating this variation

Figure 4-1. Leveraging Commonalities to Promote Variation Leveling[11]

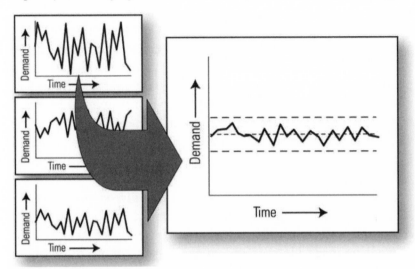

leveling effect. The graphs on the left illustrate the variation in customer demands for individual parts needed to support production
operations. Managing them individually requires some sort of
buffering, either padding production schedules or accumulating
inventories, to ensure their timely delivery despite severe uncertainty in demand. Yet these buffers represent sources of lag that respond poorly to changing circumstances. As described in Chapter 2,
despite working well within a stable environment, these actions
might break down and make matters even worse when conditions
suddenly shift.

We can see the effect of this shift on the right side of Figure 4-1;
by managing a group of items sharing common manufacturing characteristics as a single group (as is done in a mixed-model operation
commonly seen at Toyota), *their combined variation flattens out.* Managing these items together as a seamless product family effectively
dampens out the externally driven disruption that would impact performance and progress to other workstations upstream.

Making this work requires identifying opportunities for variation
leveling—not just with the end item, but throughout the creation of

value. For manufacturers, this means grouping together those elements sharing "common materials, tooling, setup procedures, labor skills, cycle time, and especially work flow or [process] routings."[12] They can be produced from beginning to end by teams working together in manufacturing cells staffed with people working as teams to turn out complete end items, components, or clearly severable portions of major operations. The ability to switch seamlessly back and forth from producing one item and then the next makes it possible to dramatically dampen the variation from changing demands of individual items, with significant effects beginning after combining just a handful of items.[13]

Performing an early assessment to identify opportunities for aligning product families in a way that optimizes the grouping of common elements is critical. It should be conducted before major changes are made, like outsourcing major elements of work, in order to keep from locking out the ability to make important shifts. Doing so will increase understanding product families as a means for promoting value stream thinking, defining them as the driving mechanisms for routing out lag. Moreover, identifying product families that promote this result farther back in the continuum of value creation stands to amplify the benefits, expanding efforts past narrow threads of savings toward creating broad webs of improvement whose benefits extend across the entire value-added map, driving down uncertainty across a wide range of activities.

Case Example: Using Product Families as the Focal Point for Driving Down Lag and Loss

As the Defense Department's largest logistics combat support agency, the Defense Logistics Agency (DLA) must overcome harsh conditions to provide supplies to meet the dynamic demands of military and civilian customers around the world. One of its challenges is obtaining spare parts for out-of-production weapons systems—aircraft, tanks, and ships, which might contain tens of thousands of parts, any of which can require replacement in order to keep a system operational. Not only are these parts critical, they tend to be very expensive.[14]

Complicating matters are low and sporadic customer demands for many of these parts, making required inventories and ordering frequencies almost impossible to accurately predict. Moreover, supplier lead time—a key measure of lag—is generally substantial; the time between placing an order and receiving parts often ranges from many months to well over a year. This means planners' already challenging jobs are complicated by the need to forecast demands that might occur well into the future, creating even greater lag. Often with no active production capability and limited inventory (it is too expensive to stock quantities of millions of unique items without solid evidence of current need), delivering what the customers need just when they need it is truly a daunting task.

One project, called Supplier Utilization Through Responsive Grouped Enterprises (SURGE), pointed to a solution. Rather than managing items individually, it sought to demonstrate the real-world applicability of product family-based groupings—sourcing together a traditionally problematic group of items (hydraulic tubes for fighter jets) as a means for creating long-term supplier relationships for overcoming these constraints. In theory, managing like items (those formed from common materials utilizing similar manufacturing methods) together would help suppliers overcome their individual uncertainties by managing them as a combined group. Their relative production interchangeability should help smooth out the overall demand pattern, creating the variation leveling effect depicted in Figure 4-1, resulting in greater predictability, lower costs, and improved product quality.

Initial results were dramatic.[15] A supplier substantially slashed its lead times—as much as two-thirds on some parts—while dramatically increasing its ability to respond to unexpected demand surges. Delivery schedules were generally met, even for selected items that experienced an unexplained demand spike of nearly 1,000 percent. And this greater responsiveness did not cost more, as one might expect. Instead, prices *dropped*, by as much as 30 percent for individual items across the family.[16]

Corporations like Cessna Aircraft Company have also attained major benefits by applying a variation of this approach. Rather than launching headfirst into new, long-term contractual arrangements that would relinquish responsibility and authority for producing their parts, components, or major assemblies to their suppliers, Cessna recognized the need to take a step back and begin by gaining a deeper understanding of the elements that go into these products.

Cessna first mapped common materials across its BOMs that could be more effectively managed together as combined groups (it refers to these as Centers of Excellence, or COEs, as described in Chapter 3), commonalities that normally would be lost among disparate supply arrangements. By creating arrangements for manufacturing cells with suppliers to produce these items together to maximize the variation smoothing benefits, it was able to slash lead times and prices and promote dramatically more reliable flow, even for some of the most challenging materials.

But Cessna goes further still, remaining engaged with its suppliers, helping to streamline their value streams. The company begins by training these suppliers in applying lean principles to gain real benefit from managing by product families. To support their efforts, Cessna makes its own flexible, low-cost raw material purchasing arrangements available. And it created a low-quantity, pull-based system to minimize the amount of inventory that must be held by Cessna and these suppliers, slashing inventory costs for each.

As of this writing, the company's results have been remarkable; some product families slashed lead times from thirteen weeks to only five days, while concurrently slashing costs by 15 to 20 percent.[17] Moreover, this new supplier base structure dramatically speeds up sourcing of new items. Since COE suppliers must openly share information about their operations and cost structure, parts can quickly be added into existing families without delays from evaluating capacity, quality, delivery, cost, and performance, factors for which its approach gives specific information and current history. By cutting sourcing time from weeks to days and providing a solid starting point for determining pricing, the company has slashed a key source of lag related to introducing new products.

By first taking a step back and rethinking how individual elements can be better combined before proceeding with process improvements or supplier arrangements, companies and institutions can achieve greater transformation than would otherwise be possible to recognize. Family sourcing can powerfully shift the way business is done, enabling companies to see across far-reaching, diverse operations, organizations, and information systems before restructuring and locking out these potential solutions.

5 Organizational Flow as the Pathway to Lean

A S A FRESHMAN IN COLLEGE, I was amazed as I gazed across the network of paved walkways across campus. What was remarkable was how astute the campus planners appeared to have been—they seemed to recognize precisely where people would walk between the university's many buildings, laying out the paths in a way that anticipated students' routes across its vast lawns. Their planning was near perfect, a feat that seemed utterly amazing.

Then a friend explained to me that this was not at all how it was done. The needed analysis would be impossible to perform, he explained; even a detailed study of class locations and student schedules would only begin to address the many considerations that would dictate the pattern where students might tread. Instead, the architects simply waited for a year and then paved over the ruts worn by the students.

The lean movement began with much the same approach—leaving wide open all possibilities and then defining specific steps after years of experimentation proved the need for a series of structured pathways. A number of tools and practices were ultimately formalized, particularly the more visible elements that the Toyota system used for finding waste and solving specific challenges. Today these have become widely recognized as the core techniques that make up a lean solution. While helpful for guiding travelers whose destinations are nearby and more straightforward, these paths fall seriously short of pointing the way for those who have farther to go.

Many companies have used these methods for successful shifts to a leaner approach, speeding production and reducing wastes. Still, it is not uncommon to see organizations plateau after reaching a steady-state level of maturity. For others, their sticking point appears to come even earlier. As described in Chapter 4, the greater the complexities of their products and operations, the more difficult it can be to gain a foothold beyond basic tools and tactics.

This is not to say that progress is not being made. On the contrary, it is truly inspiring to speak with individuals at organizations who "get it." For whatever reason, they came to see the greater art-of-the-possible that this approach represents and set themselves on course to achieve it. They recognized that targeting cost savings alone does little to keep up with changes in customer demand; that preventing backsliding takes going beyond tactical or steady-state lean, although these can contribute important capabilities along the way. They understand that increasing their ability to anticipate what customers want and then exceeding their expectations creates what turns into lasting lean success.

These are the real leaders in the lean movement. At some point in their journey the lightbulb went on; they saw their transformation as a way to not only become more efficient but to reach further toward what is really important: creating dynamic value for the customer and sustainable wealth for the corporation.

The challenge is to find a way for others to reach this realization. They must come to see that going lean means more than its first steps represent—and then set forth on a pathway to advancing beyond the intermediate plateaus toward the highest level of excellence. Doing so will take more than a grasp of the mechanics; it will take building a new mindset—the art of the possible—and then breaking down the organizational complexity that so often obscures the best pathway for advancement. This is particularly the case within industries marked by great complexity and business uncertainty.

It has once again come time to pave the pathway to reveal a systematic methodology for seeing through this complexity. And doing so supports one of the basic tenets of lean: Adopt an organizational construct that expands individuals' insights and promotes transparency and simplicity.

Simplifying Through Decentralization

In some ways, Alfred Sloan's concept of decentralized management has created an even broader impact on business than Henry Ford's moving assembly line. Sloan's approach to delegating decision making created the means for keeping GM's vast network of operations and suppliers in lockstep while GM turned out the much greater variety so critical to his strategy's success. It was his split from Ford's system of centralized control that made possible the much greater complexity that characterizes his multiproduct line approach, which launched the automaker into market leadership for decades to come.

This basic concept seems central to breaking through the vast complexity that represents perhaps the greatest challenge in advancing in lean maturity—although implemented in a much different way. It makes sense, therefore, to understand why lean decentralization differs so fundamentally, and why it serves as an important foundation to lean dynamic's tools and practices.

Value Versus Volume or Velocity

As described in Chapter 1, Sloan's application of decentralization was founded on a distinctly different mindset from that of lean dynamics. Rather than tracking the details, Sloan delegated authority to managers, who reported their results based on *average* production levels (or *standard volume*), optimizing for the enormous, predictable customer demand that represented the norm. This solved the challenge of managing GM's vast complexity—but it also brought significant limitations.

Factories came to operate well at or near the production volumes for which they were built, but these efficiencies quickly dropped when volumes shifted from anticipated conditions. Moreover, they came to require "absolutely level production—or the nearest to it that could be attained," a limitation that caused loss to skyrocket during economic downturns or demand surges.[1]

Today's supply chain solutions, intent on speeding operational ve-locity, run the risk of contributing to this effect. *Going Lean* describes the hazard of creating long-term arrangements aimed at speeding flow and reducing inventories by delegating production of major components to suppliers. Without first addressing lag that amplifies variation and disruption when conditions fluctuate, sudden surges could undermine suppliers' ability to perform, and economic down-turns can compromise their viability—a reality increasingly faced by many businesses today.[2]

Lean dynamics' very different concept of decentralization ad-dresses business complexity by applying an organizational framework that mitigates the challenge of managing its many critical details. It does not depend on simplifying assumptions to make decentralization work, as did Sloan's approach. Instead, it applies decentralization as a means for *embracing the details*, creating a structure that delegates re-sponsibility to individuals at different levels across the organization as a way for tackling complexity head-on. It restructures so that specific activities can be optimized by eliminating lag and creating dynamic dampening capabilities that prevent disruption and promote consis-tency across continually changing conditions.

The result is a much flatter value curve—a bottom-line measure of stable value across a range of volumes, reflecting not only velocity but greater agility in responding to change. Still, making this work requires making a substantial shift to create the necessary conditions so the workforce can take the lead.

Inclusion Versus Control

Perhaps what most distinguishes a lean dynamics solution is its clear split from the tradition of dealing with business's myriad, diverse ac-tivities by imposing rigid systems of top-down controls and simpli-fying assumptions (which inherently create disconnects and lag, as discussed earlier). It is a very different approach to decentralization, driven by workforce *inclusion*, where individuals across the corpora-tion or institution become integral to guiding and tracking critical as-pects of the business.

The key is breaking work into more manageable increments of value—clear elements that tangibly contribute to the final product (for an aircraft or automobile, this might be basic materials, parts, components, or other recognizable elements, as described in Chapter 4). Rather than performing discrete, disconnected processing steps, individuals with common skills and equipment can be given responsibility for producing the range of items within a given product family from beginning to end. This makes it possible to manage the details that go into everything from scheduling work to ordering materials, tightly synchronizing activities across a range of conditions, minimizing disconnects that are often the root cause of waste.

This restructuring naturally expands workers' and managers' span of insight, making it possible for them to manage the details of value creation at each step along the way—a fundamental key to its success.

Insight Versus Information

At Southwest Airlines, there is no clean split between those who measure and those who perform work. Employees remain constantly aware of the company's goals—from profit and revenue to how their work impacts the customer's needs. Each understands the larger objective of his or her work, such as the importance of ensuring on-time flight departures.

The importance of expanding worker insight in this way is critical to the company's results, as noted by Brandeis University professor Jody Hoffer Gittell in her book *The Southwest Airlines Way*.

> Interviews with Southwest frontline employees revealed they understood the overall work process—and the links between their own jobs and the jobs performed by their counterparts in other functions. When asked to explain what they were doing and why, the answers were typically couched in reference to the overall process. "The pilot has to do A, B, and C before we take off, so I need to get this to him right away."[3]

Workers' broader span of insight—a natural result of managing work from end to end for complete increments of value—helps facilitate the challenge of eliminating lag across the business by creating a much more intuitive flow of information. Moreover, it dramatically simplifies what information must be broadly shared and minimizes information disconnects that are often the root cause of lag and waste.

Perhaps the greatest benefit is creating a depth of insight that goes far beyond what could be captured in an information system. Individuals performing or managing work to produce items from beginning to end across a product family are able to see not only the individual process steps but the challenges and opportunities for improvement that exist between these activities. They find themselves in a position to identify improvements to supplied materials, design details, or even manufacturing equipment that can streamline their activities or produce a more consistent or superior product. The result is greater consistency, precision, and innovation—even when conditions do not remain stable and predictable.

Case Example: The Benefits of Breaking Through Traditional Barriers

Consider the approach taken by the Pittsburgh Regional Health Initiative (PRHI), a nonprofit consortium of healthcare providers in southwestern Pennsylvania. More than a decade ago PRHI embarked on an ambitious program to apply lean principles as a means of overcoming serious problems with the healthcare system. It wasn't hard to see that a problem existed, with outright failures like hospital infections and medication errors affecting millions of patients across the nation, costing billions of dollars per year. The startling fact that preventable medical mistakes have become a leading cause of death itself makes clear the critical need for change.[4]

Through education, research fellowships, and awareness-building efforts, PRHI is clearly intent on tackling this challenge head-on. Rather than simply addressing whatever problem comes up first (as some lean consultants had apparently advised) or emphasizing peripheral administrative areas, its network of medical providers pursue projects directly targeting "a clinical objective," from hospital infections to medication errors—addressing some of the most serious challenges affecting patients' well-being. So far the results have been promising—from slashing hospital infection rates, preventing mistakes from patient "handoffs" between units or across work shifts, and reducing medication errors or delays.[5]

Its focus is not so much on creating technology-based solutions; its participants' efforts have repeatedly demonstrated that even simple, low-tech practices can have profound impact.[6] Much of their attention instead goes to challenges like breaking through organizational barriers across this vast, complex, and continually changing system. "So much is done in isolation," says PRHI's president and CEO, Dr. Karen Wolk Feinstein. Solutions must come from correcting this, creating transparency across the entire system, leading to real value in the form of quality services, providing care that is always effective, safe, and efficient.

One of the more recent examples of success in advancing this vision is Pharmacy Agents for Change, a program that targets the enormous problem of delivering proper doses of the right medications to patients when they are needed. By breaking through traditional organizational barriers, making changes like including pharmacists in hospital treatment teams, participants improved everything from preventing drug interactions to increasing patients' reliability in taking their prescribed medications, in one case reducing discrepancies (such as illegible, duplicate, or out-of-date prescriptions) from as much as 90 percent to less than 10 percent (a statistic that continues to improve).[7]

Creating and implementing transformational solutions requires applying these changes not just across departments but between institutions. As Dr. Feinstein explains, a chronically ill patient may receive care from a wide range of facilities that provide everything from skilled nursing to cardiology or other specialties, mental health services, and primary care. This vast range of paths that can be different for every patient creates tremendous opportunities for disconnects—each of which can lead to inefficiency and errors, affecting the system and ultimately the patient.

PRHI's efforts point to important lessons that seem to be gaining acceptance. Broadly extending them will involve applying its structured approach along with the right incentives to promote necessary collaboration and deliberate action across broad networks of providers.

Establishing Organizational Flow

When businesses and institutions learn about lean, they tend to immediately take aim at tangible work steps to improve their flow of material and information. The reason seems clear: This physical progression of steps is easiest to visualize, making needed actions clear and direct. Beginning this way, however, neglects a critical focus proven by lean dynamics benchmarks like Toyota and Southwest Airlines: smoothing *organizational flow*.

What is organizational flow? Better known as the flow of people and process, it represents the means for optimally engaging the workforce—breaking through traditional barriers and extending workers' spans of insight so they can become instrumental in guiding these efforts.[8] Innovative industrial engineer Shigeo Shingo, who helped create the famed Toyota Production System, explained this "flow of people" as essentially how individuals coordinate and understand a broader range of steps to optimize the way in which work is done.[9]

Recognizing the Disconnects

It is common for lean efforts to begin by conducting *kaizen* events, multiday, facilitated events in which workers are taken away from their normal activities to brainstorm ways in which work can be streamlined. Yet this approach can backfire, as seems to have been the case during some of GE's "workouts" (a variant of this concept), as described by Robert Slater in *Jack Welch and the GE Way*.

It became fashionable to launch assaults against bureaucracy. But the bureaucracy had been erected in many cases to help impose discipline that assured the quality of products and processes. All too often, the assault on bureaucracy had the effect of getting rid of some of that discipline.[10]

What caused such a disconnect? Although it might seem that removing bureaucracy will correct problems like sluggish decision making, doing so can undermine traditionally managed organizations that depend on this type of structure. Participants' ability to understand this, however, is often limited by their span of insight. Although individuals can quickly hone in on *what* the problems are, they do not have sufficient understanding and visibility to see *how* to correct them.

Peter Senge referred to this as the *learning dilemma*: "We learn best from experience but we never directly experience the consequences of many of our most important decisions," he explained.[11] Why is this? As corporations grew to enormous proportions over the last century, they lost the organizational simplicity, transparency, and adaptability that marked their decision making. The division of responsibilities that became so central to the way they managed their increasing scale also became a critical weakness, making it impossible for workers and managers to see the results of everything from work activities to improvement initiatives.

The more complex the organization, the more pronounced this disconnect can become, since so many decisions cross departmental lines. Workers and managers find themselves responding largely to output-based requirements and lagging metrics dictated by other divisions, often with little insight into why these are needed or what the impact of deviations that will inevitably occur might be.

Correcting this requires expanding the workforce's span of insight sufficiently to eliminate these disconnects *before* broadly involving them. This includes changing how people at different workstations and even management departments relate to one another—shifting from a fragmented structure marked by internally focused metrics, inefficient coordination, and suboptimal decision making to creating the means to gain meaningful insight into how their work relates to the final product.

Expanding the Span of Insight

Those organizations that succeed in leaping beyond existing plateaus to new levels of performance seem to create a methodology that progressively advances this span of insight. Rather than seeking to shift their organizational structure all at once, it seems important to progressively focus attention on shifting key areas with the potential to broadly affect lag (described in Chapter 4), concentrating on one part of the problem at a time. Breaking down the problem in this way—restructuring around these focal points to expand project teams' end-to-end understanding of the challenge—stands to promote the broader span of insight needed to wade through the details across complex functions and fundamentally rethink how business is done.

Chapter 7 suggests an iterative approach that identifies key focal points, extends individuals' span of insight, and implements solutions. In this way, project by project, businesses and institutions can expand their workforce's visibility by concentrating on those areas where transformation is needed and the likelihood of acceptance is greatest.

Identifying these focal points is an excellent starting point because it reveals major areas where disconnects exist and relates them to major challenges to advancement that might not have been evident to the company (or at least not documented as a priority for action). Creating specific actions for correcting these serves as a powerful opportunity to shatter traditional functional barriers—engaging people from across different functional elements to define specific actions and sequencing their implementation to increasingly expand their ability to turn out desired results.

Unlike so many *kaizen* events, this is not a once-and-out exercise where changes are quickly made and then attention is shifted elsewhere. Instead, it takes continuous improvement beyond generic philosophy, concentrating iterative, incremental advancement at key focus areas with clear objectives for attaining tangible, bottom-line outcomes. The specific manner in which organizations accomplish this will vary; the key, however, seems to be assembling cross-functional action teams responsible for progressively fostering an expanding shift within selected focus areas (described in Chapter 7).

Bit by bit, individuals' span of insight will expand, enabling them to see across disconnects to identify high-potential solutions. When given the necessary insight and tools to succeed, individuals seem willing and able to take the lead in restructuring the flow of work, information, decision making, and innovation—to succeed in stimulating lean transformation like never before.

Key Point: Shifting Focus from Processes to Products

Many people familiar with lean methods recognize their emphasis on creating manufacturing cells: a way of structuring work so that individuals in a work unit perform the entire set of actions needed to turn out complete products or components from beginning to end (increments of value, as described in Chapter 4; typically product families share common characteristics). This is a powerful way of shifting to a product-oriented focus, emphasizing the deliberate creation of value, rather than shifting processing steps for local gains without specifically understanding how this impacts the final product or the customer. Aligning workers can be a powerful force to:

- **Create a sense of ownership.** Making workers responsible for the end-to-end production of tangible products leads to greater insight into, understanding of, and enthusiasm for the work they perform. This tends to create a much stronger sense of pride and ownership.

- **Relate work to a specific customer.** Creating ownership for tangible units makes it possible for more meaningful coordination with suppliers and customers (individuals representing upstream or downstream operational steps). This relationship has proven effective in developing the ability to better anticipate and respond to dynamic challenges, such as sudden changes or surges in demand.

- **Serve as a focal point for meaningful measurement of improvement.** Workers' increased awareness of the disconnects between value-creating steps makes it possible to create meaningful, actionable metrics they can monitor

and act on to keep flow progressing smoothly and efficiently, mitigating lag and accumulation of waste and
keeping them out over time.

■ **Promote innovation.** Some organizations allow these cells
to operate as "semiautonomous units," permitting them to
make significant adjustments and exercise creativity in improving product flow, stocking supplies, and reducing inventories. Workers develop suggestions and build business
cases (with the help of their own financial analysts); when
approved, management acts quickly to approve requested
funds, making sometimes significant changes in how they
do business.[12]

In this chapter we have seen the importance of decentralizing management to break through the organizational complexity that would
otherwise stand in the way of attaining broad-based transformation.
Lean dynamics seeks to accomplish this by realigning the business to
promote real ownership at each point along the way.

The result can be a series of product families managed in a
largely decentralized manner (rigorously integrated into the overall
system, as described in Chapter 7), in which workers optimize their
performance based on a specific understanding of what their customers need. This promotes a greater span of insight into what it
takes to create their elements of value, as well as how they fit into the
broader value-creating structure, making it possible for workers to
take a lead role in mitigating lag, holding down waste, and optimizing results even under continually changing demands.

The chapters in this section have explored key elements that form
the pathway for advancing to higher levels of lean maturity: recognizing
the elements of value that can focus implementation efforts and creating the organizational structuring that will drive the needed change. We
are now ready to explore where to begin such an effort: identifying the
transformational focal points that can point the way to where businesses and institutions might begin their journey or refocusing efforts
that have already begun to gain the greatest advantage from these methods, in a way that promotes ongoing advancement in lean maturity.

CHAPTER

6 Targeting Transformation

FOR MORE THAN half a century Dr. Shigeo Shingo has been acknowledged as an engineering genius for his contributions in creating and disseminating the benefits of the Toyota Production System. Today, with a major award bearing his name, this recognition seems destined to continue.[1] Yet, despite all of the fanfare, his methods seem generally misunderstood; the general focus of many lean initiatives today appears to be drifting away from the underlying intent of his teachings.

Shingo's attention was not so much on addressing widespread inefficiencies; instead, his focus seemed to be on advancing key elements making possible deeper aspects of lean transformation. One major emphasis was on speeding equipment *changeovers*—he took aim at slashing the time it took to shift equipment from producing one part to begin producing another.

Equipment changeover was clearly a significant constraint to production activities at the time; automobile manufacturers routinely took an entire day to remove and replace the dies used in stamping body panels. This drove factories to operate using extended production runs to absorb the cost of this downtime, producing large batches of identical items before changing over again—*economic quantities they sent to storage until needed.* Shingo focused on slashing changeover times (in conjunction with managing by product family, as described in Chapter 4) as a means to drive down the need for these large batch sizes and permit factories to produce in quantities that more closely matched actual demands.

Going Lean described how this very different focus transformed Toyota's production approach; slashing changeover times was instrumental to creating such recognizable lean benefits as quicker deliveries, lower inventories, higher quality (in part from reduced changeover errors), greater productivity due to less downtime for people and equipment, and greater flexibility for meeting changing customer needs.

Central to making this approach work was Toyota's relentless pursuit of waste reduction—not as a general means for cutting costs (as it is often applied today), but as a targeted emphasis to support key shifts like reduced changeover times.[2] By restructuring setup activities and eliminating excesses of all types, Toyota was ultimately able to cut its major setups from several hours to around three minutes.[3]

Creating Solutions, Not Chasing Problems

Today, waste reduction seems to have become the mantra of much of the business literature, as evidenced by the proliferation of problem-solving tools that corporations and institutions hasten to adopt. Corporations and institutions are quick to embrace this—perhaps because of its intuitive benefit to how they operate today. But, as we have seen, making real progress comes from applying these techniques not to target a specific problem or desired outcome but to *create transformational shifts for progressively advancing in maturity.*

This realization first hit me more than a decade ago while I searched for lessons during my study of manufacturing improvement methods for the Joint Strike Fighter Program. On the surface, the results in applying improvements ranging from lean to Six Sigma techniques seemed broadly successful. Most slashed huge amounts of waste from activities ranging from materials management through assembly; production times were down nearly across the board, as were inventory levels. And for many of the participants, improvements were dramatic—as much as 67 and 80 percent, respectively.[4]

Yet, in spite of their success in waste reduction, only a small number demonstrated as significant of results when it came to reducing their bottom-line costs. Although things *seemed* to be moving in the right direction, these discrete fixes did not add up to the expected results.

A handful of factories stood apart. They went beyond implementing lean tools as tactics aimed at correcting discrete workstations or narrowly defined value streams—beyond the targeted problem solving that seems typical of improvement efforts. Instead, they advanced by progressively addressing an underlying condition that affected their overall results: their *cycle time variation*, or the deviations in time it took to assemble each successive unit off the line (depicted in Figure 3-1). Doing this, it turned out, was the key to attaining powerful, bottom-line cost savings.

Figure 6-1 illustrates the severe state of internal variation my study team found affected one factory (a result that does not seem to be atypical in this industry). The chart depicts its problem: substantial cycle time variation—wide swings in the time it took to build each successive unit, deviating as much as 30 percent from the average.

Figure 6-1. Example of Cycle Time Variation in Aerospace⁵

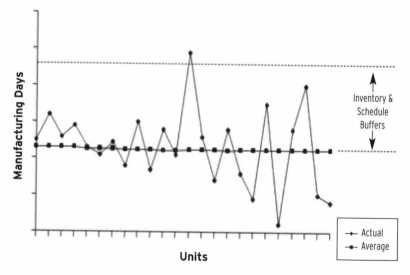

Why is this important? The study showed that the turmoil this represents undermines a factory's ability to operate efficiently—driving up inventories and extending production schedules, compromising operational predictability. As described in Chapter 1, workarounds to standard procedures create a greater potential for errors, requiring additional inspections and bookkeeping to ensure critical defects do not escape (particularly critical in producing aircraft because of the criticality of protecting flight safety). And the uncertainty this causes has an amplifying effect up and down the line, impacting scheduling or causing workarounds in the many shops and suppliers feeding the component items that support these operations.

Those companies that had achieved the greatest results stood out in that they made great progress in addressing this cycle time variation—going beyond applying lean methods as part of a scattershot approach to creating tactical fixes, instead stabilizing their operations by first improving their management of basic elements like production and inventory control capabilities. Only after freeing up the basic bottlenecks that choked the progression of their activities did the more recognizable lean tools (e.g., statistical measurement tools, value stream realignment, advanced supplier relationships, or enhanced product designs) generate substantial results. Taking actions that progressively addressed this underlying driver for real improvement led to the most significant bottom-line savings.[6]

Knowingly or not, these facilities had come up with a powerful solution addressing a core *transformational focus*—creating a baseline for stability before advancing to more recognizable lean practices by successively addressing the greatest drivers for mitigating uncertainty and disruption, a critical challenge facing their business. Their structured advancement demonstrated the potential to save as much as 25 percent of the cost of producing an aircraft. Perhaps more importantly, their results showed that for implementing lean activities, a natural progression does exist.[7]

Identifying Focal Points for Transformation

We have seen that advancing in lean maturity takes breaking objectives into manageable focal points and addressing them through a structured progression of activities. For aerospace manufacturing, mitigating cycle time variation and creating a baseline for predictable operational flow proved to be the essential initial focal point.

But how can companies attain this? My research identified the need for a structured approach consisting of a progression of actions that first create a baseline of stability (such as improving inventory accuracy and production control to make the right materials available when needed), reducing workarounds, and permitting more recognizable lean tools to become most productive (as shown in Figure 6-2).

This same general structure can point the way for other industries to progressively address core challenges they must overcome to advance in lean maturity. A hospital, for instance, might begin by identifying the core drivers it must address—substantial factors like infections or unpredictable patient loading that have the greatest impact on short- and long-term objectives for optimizing patient care. Developing a progressive structure for addressing immediate challenges can build the stable foundation needed to progressively move forward with actions offering increasing benefits.

After creating a more stable foundation, the next activities might concentrate on key dynamic drivers affecting their value creation; perhaps addressing long supplier lead times that might cause little impact during stable demand, but create enormous challenges when

Figure 6-2. A Hierarchy for Progressing with Lean Implementation[8]

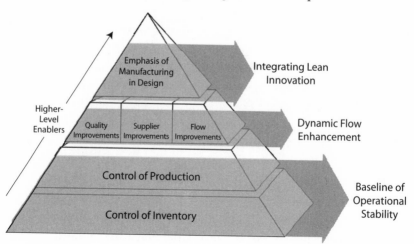

conditions suddenly shift. Actions that begin with more tactical measures like collaborating to hold long-lead materials or components (intended as a temporary means for addressing key drivers of operational lag, described in Chapter 7) might advance to more dynamic solutions at this phase. Assembling cross-functional action teams responsible for progressively fostering an expanded shift (described in Chapter 5) can promote solutions such as combining elements into product families to smooth out variation and broadly address these challenges. The structure this provides for understanding the nature of value from end to end offers a powerful platform to define and manage follow-on activities and create significant impact on these core areas, optimizing progress while lowering resistance to change and progressively addressing the steepness of their value curve.

Adopting such a structure for addressing specifically defined focal points creates a powerful means for breaking from the tool-based, problem-solving mindset that leads to fragmented results and acts as a barrier to advancing in lean maturity. But for many managers and executives, this application can be difficult, because it means rethinking actions and fully thinking through the underlying changes they intend to achieve before launching into lean improvement projects.

Leading with Metrics

One of the greatest challenges in implementing business transformation efforts is determining a clear way to measure results. Many organizations progress using outdated performance measures; despite identifying a new focus aimed at better supporting customers, they might cling to internally focused metrics that measure average process performance—causing well-intentioned lean efforts to end up improving internal efficiencies without a clear way of tracing them to the objective of maximizing product value that they set out to achieve.

Perhaps the root of the problem is that most of today's improvement programs quickly shift attention away from any tangible way of tracking value. After becoming sold on the need to apply information technology, business process reengineering, or Lean Six Sigma, organizations quickly seek to identify and implement improvements to processing steps. Yet, in complex operations, it can be difficult to relate processing changes to tangible improvements in customer value. This represents a fundamental source of lag—one that must be corrected as an integral part of shifting to a leaner way of doing business.

Going Lean introduced a concept for more specifically measuring value: using the value curve to assess a business's or an institution's creation of products and services in response to changing customer demands and business conditions. This proved to be a powerful measure for gauging companies' bottom-line performance, distinguishing lean organizations from the others. It stands to reason that this same approach can be applied to measuring performance for individual products at different stages of value creation (applied to their major increments of value, described in Chapter 4), or even as a means for gauging responsiveness to the needs of specific customers (mapping customer-specific value curves). This offers a direct means for assessing a company's (or its suppliers') effectiveness in improving value at various stages in its creation, eliminating a key source of lag in tracking progress with lean improvement initiatives.

However, it is also important to identify interim checkpoints to keep improvement efforts from falling off course along the way. These offer the means to track incremental progress, sustaining focus and enthusiasm throughout what might otherwise seem to be the endless pursuit of an elusive goal.

But what should constitute such checkpoints? To answer this, consider the challenge of building a cross-country railroad. A straight-line approach to assessing progress across a three-dimensional landscape does not begin to describe reality; it would miss all of the hidden effort that goes into accommodating a challenging terrain. Similarly, much of the progress toward implementing lean dynamics goes beyond what is seen on the surface; much of what is done goes to building a foundation for overcoming business obstacles rather than addressing them head-on. Measurements must therefore focus on advancing not only those results that can be clearly seen but also the less-visible elements involved in creating an optimal solution.

Cycle time variation (described earlier in this chapter) offers one such checkpoint. As a key indication of flow disruption, high cycle time variation points to areas within the value-added map where lag is likely to be significant—areas where taking action can create the greatest benefit. Thus, it can serve as a metric to help identify transformational focal points and track progress toward improvement (in conjunction with such traditional measures as inventories and cycle time, which together proved in my aerospace study to be the indicator of greatest success in addressing loss).

Beginning with strong, well-designed metrics is a critical follow-on to the dynamic value assessment. Together they bring greater consistency and clarity to a direction that might otherwise not be so evident within the fragmented structure within which most must begin. This can help managers reach forward in a consistent direction even as their span of insight continues to grow, mitigating the need for them to mandate arbitrary quotas that do not necessarily contribute to intended results.

Key Point: The Illuminating Nature of Metrics

There is tremendous wisdom in the old expression *What you measure is what you get*. Organizations are often amazed by what they can achieve by using metrics to shine a light on what is truly important.

■ **Keep it simple.** Often businesses create too many metrics, overwhelming managers with information, with the result that none stands out as important. Creating a few that focus on the top-level vision (relating directly to the value curve), with others that tie this directly to the focal points for localized initiatives (such as cycle time variation) supported by specific supporting objectives (e.g., lead times, cost, and quality), can help create a greater focus on what is important for substantial progress.

■ **Balance bottom-line metrics.** Focusing on several interrelated metrics at once helps avoid results that resemble what happens when one side of a balloon is squeezed—things tighten up where attention is focused but not without causing things to simply shift to other areas that are not tightly controlled.

- **Measure at all levels within the organization.** Delegating responsibility for measurement and oversight to those who are closest to the action is critical to minimizing complexity. Not only does this contribute to expanding the workforce's span of insight, but it reduces the complexity of coordinating information and enables decision making at the appropriate levels in the organization—key factors in mitigating lag.

- **Track interim conditions that support bottom-line metrics.** Tracking is essential for multiphased projects, ensuring that the workforce understands that even the less visible advances are essential to the progression to lean maturity.

- **Create execution transparency.** Metrics must relate to bottom-line results, ensuring that changes create real improvements for both the customer and the corporation.

Transforming from the Top

Most business management books will tell you that real transformation must begin by attaining support from top management for what lies ahead. But too often, support seems superficial; after the initial sales pitch, management might agree to hire consultants to manage the tasks involved, enabling themselves to move on to more pressing matters.

Yet, it is hard to imagine matters more worthy of executives' attention than guiding the bottom-up transformation of their businesses.

Perhaps the reason so many managers disengage from the details is the belief that such efforts can be managed as so many operational tasks are today: as standardized activities whose benefits will inevitably reach the bottom line. We have seen, however, that implementing lean is far from standardized; businesses and institutions must develop their own strategies to fill their existing gaps, creating a pathway that suits their unique challenges, constraints, strategies, and values. These cannot come from hired consultants, or even from middle managers; choosing the direction at critical junctures must come straight from the top.

Those at the highest levels of management must therefore lead in developing a deliberately planned, well-constructed, and tightly measured progression of activities to advance their organization in lean maturity. Their continued engagement is critical for maneuvering its complex, changing pathways, responding to the evolving insights and changing conditions that will emerge during the course of its implementation.

As we saw in Chapter 5, while leadership is critical, the workforce is central to identifying and executing the transformational shifts necessary for going lean. Leaders must engage and empower their people, beginning with their middle managers, not just superficially, but in a way that lets them truly become a core part of the new solution.

Breaking Through the Hierarchy

Perhaps the greatest role that managers must serve is creating the right culture to support real transformation. They must lead the way by clearly and consistently communicating the reasons for the shift, reiterating core points from the case for change, and continually reaching out to reassure people who are undoubtedly concerned about their future with the corporation. What is perhaps most important, however, is demonstrating that all staff are part of this solution—that management, too, is affected—and that this will create opportunities for the business and its people.

Management functions, like production activities, tend to be split into specific areas of responsibility. This creates an emphasis that tends to be introspective; managers might focus attention on improving activities that appear to make things work better but in reality add no meaningful benefit to the bottom line. Such a fragmented approach tends to reinforce existing disconnects; it can increase lag, actually undermining a company's or an institution's progress toward creating a lean solution.

What can be done? Organizations and institutions can embrace the decentralization principles of lean dynamics (described in Chapter 5) and break through natural divisions within the management hierarchy to promote decision making that will be much less bu-

reaucratic to better support the goal of creating smooth organizational flow. Breaking down a steep hierarchy and delegating more authority downward is important to streamlining decision making and
simplifying information flow, each of which is critical to speeding the
flow of solutions and ideas.

For decades, experts have understood the need for making this
shift in organizational structure a core part of going lean "so that job
responsibility, information linkages, and reporting relationships will
not hamper its progress."9 Yet making such a shift is far from trivial;
it takes breaking down traditional organizational barriers and establishing an action team with improved linkages to facilitate the
deeper analysis and innovation needed for crafting farther-reaching
solutions. And this requires reaching an understanding with the leaders of each of the affected divisions, who must accept that they must
lose top employees to another team.

A first step toward restructuring might be creating a steering
committee—a decision-making forum to include from the outset all
major stakeholders across the enterprise in structuring for the lean
transformation. This serves as a means to expand decision makers'
insight, growing their buy-in and understanding as the movement
continues to mature. This can be vital to making the organizational
shifts that are so critical to driving real transformation, such as pop-
ulating improvement teams with the right resources and making
process changes that will likely span the traditional boundaries of
many parts of the organization. It also brings top experts with the
broadest span of insight together to validate its direction at major decision points along the way.

The way in which this committee is structured is particularly important; adequate inclusion and ground rules can make the difference between creating great benefit or serious liability. Furthermore,
corporations and institutions should consider bringing in labor at the
outset; at some point along the way, they might consider including
suppliers and, after progressing past the tactical to the dynamic levels
of maturity, might also consider bringing in customers once a basic
level of stability has been achieved.

Another important aspect for the committee to consider is how to encourage employee participation in lean dynamics efforts. For instance, it is important to create organizational mechanisms that make clear that a lean dynamics role is not a path to obscurity, but one that will lead the way to future opportunities. This is critical if the best and the brightest are to be drawn away from traditional, prestigious areas of specialty with known career paths.

Embracing Criticism

Some lean experts indicate that one of the greatest barriers to going lean is the widespread resistance of middle management. They suggest that these managers simply do not want their jobs changed; others say that they need more training. Almost universally, the problem is presumed to rest with those who resist—that lack of real progress is somehow their fault because they simply oppose change.

But when so many front-line leaders raise a concern, wouldn't it make sense to first understand the basis for their concerns before writing them off? This is where top leadership has the opportunity to become engaged; rather than discouraging important insights, they can encourage feedback from their cadre of middle managers, whose clearer vantage points might offer valuable insights that can improve their direction or keep their efforts from stumbling.

This is precisely what I tried to do. As I traveled the country following the release of *Going Lean*, I spoke with many individuals who expressed real concern about what they had been asked to do. They seemed to have valid concerns—for one, that implementing lean at one facility could mean something strikingly different at another. Most convinced me they had their organizations' best interests in mind and seemed passionate about driving change—but for all this time, effort, and expense, he or she demanded *real* improvement, without creating new problems.

Some were charged with searching out anything that could be claimed as "lean," filling out spreadsheets with as many "savings" as they could to prove the program's success. Others cringed as lean teams established rules that eliminated meetings or other activities deemed "wasteful" because they did not directly impact the customer. While not all examples were this extreme, it was not hard to see why individuals involved in this had become frustrated, and I could not help but share in their concern.

Why, then, wouldn't their leaders listen? If a central part of going lean is embracing the insights of the workforce, wouldn't these companies want to learn as much as they could from their front-line managers, individuals entrusted with making things happen that really matter?

Years ago I was shocked by the seemingly counterintuitive way a manager dealt with a different sort of critical feedback, expressing outright excitement when a customer survey showed a sharp *increase in negative feedback*. How could he see this as *good* news? The answer was simple. In the past, he explained, customers had no reason to believe that their concerns would be acted on. Subsequently, however, his organization had changed; it began taking deliberate, visible action to address their complaints. Since customers could now see real evidence of interest, they knew their input would make a difference. The bottom line was that *they now cared enough to explain what they really thought*.

This is a critical tenet in transforming to lean; stakeholders of all sorts, inside and outside of the organization, must feel free to give their insights. They must come to care enough to do so because they believe that their feedback will be valued. For an approach founded on the contributions of its people, this should be the cornerstone for action. Yet it is perhaps the most frequent failure, causing well-intentioned people with solid insights to hold their tongues rather than risk severe backlash.

So, in a way, it appears that middle management resistance is more of an *outcome* of poor guidance and leadership than the problem itself. How then should leaders respond? They should listen to their managers who are particularly well positioned to recognize any disconnects between objectives and measurements. They must look for ways to include their managers and encourage them to offer insights and to incorporate those insights into their methodologies and solutions in meaningful ways.

Rather than discouraging them, a key focus should be enabling them, looking for ways to expand their spans of insight—helping them to create solutions truly aimed at transforming end-to-end value creation for the corporation and the customer.

Key Point: Selecting *Transformational* Focal Points

A central driver to lean success is selecting the right focal point for transformation. Yet selecting these focal points depends on reaching beyond the narrow insights of managers limited by compartmentalized organizations. These focal points must reflect not only what is truly important to the business but the effect of these challenges on the customer.

Consider a common area of focus today: speeding up contract awards and creating long-term supplier arrangements. Each brings intuitive benefits to the procurement organization that will likely lead these efforts, slashing its workload and increasing its measures of productivity. But for a large organization with vast numbers of supplied items to address, where should it begin? A common recommendation is to concentrate on the much smaller number of items that analysis often shows makes up a large percentage of the total volume. Focusing on these, it seems, will naturally yield the greatest benefits to the customer and the corporation because of their contribution to sales volume.

From a lean dynamics perspective, however, their attention to these high sales volume items might not be the best avenue to cost reduction and customer results.

Think of organizations like the one described in Chapter 4, charged with supplying customers with critical items whose demand is low and uncertain but whose impact can be enormous. As described in the case study, demand uncertainty makes it difficult to stock the right number of items to meet their customers' needs, and their enormous lead times mean that incorrect forecasts will substantially impact their customers. By taking aim at this tremendous source of lag and uncertainty (e.g., restructuring to manage these items as product families for the variation smoothing effect illustrated in Figure 4-1), they can substantially increase predictability, while cutting lead times. The result can be twofold: slashing costs while driving up the ability to respond to customer needs.

Conversely, even substantial improvements for items whose demand is already fairly stable might have only a limited effect on their inventories (which are already fairly small and deterministic); since these tend to be widely available, their risk of stock-outs is already low. Moreover, while their individual sales quantity may be high, they might represent only a fraction of the range of items their customers need. Thus, from a product support standpoint, even a positive result can be far smaller when viewed from the perspective of the customers' needs.

Analysis of customer orders can reveal other potential focal points. For example, some important customers may disproportionately demand very short response times, stressing the company's ability to respond. Collaborating with these customers might give some insight into the reasons for such orders, perhaps reducing the high costs associated with urgent shipping (which can be an extraordinary cost driver). And, as described in Chapter 9, the resulting trust that this relationship will likely build can lead to further opportunities for new business down the line.

The difference seems clear. Rather than focusing on first-level issues that might produce limited results and have little impact on the customer, businesses and institutions can direct their efforts toward addressing greater sources of lag to produce greater impact on the customer and create the opportunity for much greater cost savings across a wide range of conditions.

PART

3 In Pursuit of Sustainable Excellence

W HAT BUSINESSES AND INSTITUTIONS need today is a repeatable structure for advancing in their lean dynamics journey, from initial concept to its highest level of maturity. They need a methodology that will guide them to reach beyond the temporary gains that so often mark the beginning of the journey—through the challenges that can thwart progress at each level along the way.

Chapter 7 suggests a structure that can be applied at any level of progress and reapplied once new progress is made. Chapter 8 describes how innovation must be advanced not as a separate entity, as is so often done, but integrated as part of an overarching lean dynamics transformation. Chapter 9 takes this idea a step further, describing the importance of reaching out with new products and services that meet the actual, the anticipated, and even the unrecognized demands of the marketplace, allowing organizations to respond quickly, beyond what the competition can deliver. It describes how those that advance to the highest levels of lean maturity establish a strong connection between what it is that their customers seek and their own ability to deliver it across its broad continuum of circumstances. In doing so, they become increasingly able to create new opportunities, a key to sustaining and advancing value even in challenging circumstances.

Shifting from traditional ways of thinking is central to advancing in lean maturity, which is a theme explored in Chapter 10. It describes how setting a course toward a sustainable lean capability from the outset is critical to creating and sustaining this focus and keeping efforts from plateauing at lower maturity levels and to advancing through the challenges to the tremendous possibilities that can result.

7 Taking Action

M ANY YEARS AGO I was shocked as a manager related his inclination to "err on the side of action," despite facing significant unknowns. This contradicted all that I had been taught as an aerospace engineer. As my career progressed, I grew to see that this manager's inclination to charge ahead in the face of unresolved challenges was far from unique—particularly within the realm of process improvement.

This propensity to leap to action might have something to do with how directly efforts will affect the bottom-line value. For instance, it seems rare within engineering design functions, where the impact is clear and direct. Problems with configuration or functionality will directly affect quality, cost, reliability, and customer satisfaction. Conversely, lean projects within large businesses and institutions can be introduced in a way that is so peripheral to the core of the business that interruptions pose little immediate risk. This means the consequences of making mistakes will be less severe. It also means that results can have far less meaning.

Perhaps this is why managers seem willing to launch into their lean efforts with little up-front analysis of the specific impact these might have on their business. Many seem to emphasize trial and error as the means for adapting lean principles to their own particular circumstances. Yet, this can create turmoil, which can lead to loss of workforce support (described in Chapter 5). Moreover, it likely contributes to the tremendous potential for firms and institutions to quickly plateau after attaining initial gains.

What is important, then, is creating an approach for advancement that permits flexibility for experimentation, but does so in a structured manner, focusing on the key aspects of implementing lean dynamics described throughout this book: following a consistent vision, creating attainable focal points, and advancing through organizational decentralization.

An Iterative Cycle to Advancement

Consider the advantages offered by an iterative approach to advancement, in which a cycle of assessment, focus, action, and measurement progressively increases a business's lean capabilities. Guided by an overarching vision and objectives and structured with decision points for evaluating progress and prioritizing the next steps for optimizing progress, such an approach offers the needed flexibility while maintaining rigor and focus through each phase along the way.[1]

Figure 7-1 proposes such a structure for guiding the lean dynamics journey. The core of this transformation cycle is a *dynamic value assessment*—the critical step of sorting through a business's or an institution's operations, determining the best starting point for advancing their creation of value within real challenges of its business environment (described in Appendix A). It establishes the foundation for the activities that will follow; in particular, *identifying transformation focal points*—a key to focusing improvements in a deliberate direction based on the current capabilities and needs of the business (as described in Chapter 6). Transformation begins by establishing cross-functional teams with the span of insight for identifying and managing specific solutions to advance these focal points (*promoting organizational flow*, described in Chapter 5). Next comes *implementing the shift*. Finally, since actions should produce broad-based benefits, it is important to *stabilize* the restructured activities to validate the extent of results.

Figure 7-1. Lean Dynamics Transformation Cycle

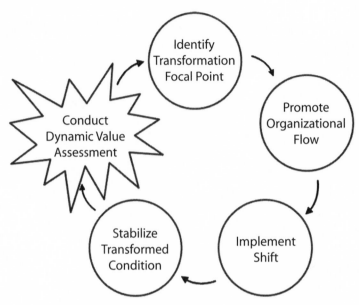

The cycle continues with follow-on analyses intended to reveal the next tier of transformational focal points, which begins the cycle all over again. Each repetition of the cycle should help drive the company or institution farther along its journey to lean maturity.

A key advantage is that this structure can be applied at any level of progress and then reapplied once new progress is made, enabling businesses or institutions to advance beyond their current plateau, overcoming common vulnerabilities and addressing a broad array of critical challenges. It permits flexibility but avoids constant drift as improvements are incorporated across the business. And it introduces improvements in a tightly coordinated manner—just as is seen at lean benchmarks—synchronizing changes with ongoing operations in a way that mitigates any disruption that might introduce waste.

Conducting follow-on dynamic value analyses at each iteration (as depicted in Figure 7-1) is critical to sustaining the momentum and revealing that far more is left to be accomplished. Additional challenges, new focal points, and refined objectives and opportunities will likely become visible through increasingly specific measurements, greater baseline stability, and the progression of capabilities.

Each new assessment creates the need to decide on new paths and projects; this offers a chance to engage the steering committee (described in Chapter 6), whose involvement, ideas, and enthusiasm can reinforce the mindset that going lean must represent more than discrete, continual improvements. Each cycle can help drive the organization toward greater levels of lean maturity as it ultimately moves up the continuum introduced in Chapter 3 (depicted in Figure 7-2).

Recognition that advancement is marked by distinct levels of maturity, marking common levels of understanding, capability, and progress, is critical to this cycle to advancement. Not only does this understanding serve to highlight the stages of the journey ahead, but it helps reveal the limiting mindset that drives so many to become complacent and fail to progress after reaching these distinct plateaus along the way. Moreover, it is important to recognize that only when organizations reach the upper levels of maturity do they seem to attain a distinct change in their value curves. This points to a real need for overcoming the challenges to reaching this critical destination in the lean journey.

Figure 7-2. Levels of Lean Maturity

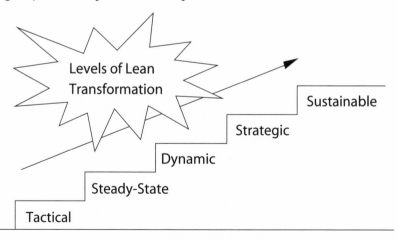

Advancing Up the Levels of Lean Maturity

How, then, can this cycle to improvement help to overcome the plateaus in advancing in lean maturity? The unfortunate reality is that many companies and institutions do not progress beyond the first steps to a dynamic lean approach, and fewer still pursue a course of strategic lean (as evidenced by the limited examples of flat value curves that mark this level of maturity). Without a structured approach to advancement, it is easy to stagnate, focusing on perfecting their capabilities at each plateau along the way rather than on implementing transformative efforts that stretch toward more advanced levels of maturity.

As shown at the base of Figure 7-2, many organizations plateau without making any lean shifts at all. They apply popular tools and techniques, from information technology to process improvements and supplier downsizing, for the purpose of cutting costs to better deal with the increasing stresses of today's business environment. Such an approach has become popular, presumably because of its relative simplicity and rapid results. Managers can simply delegate individual initiatives to different project managers, who can lead their initiatives with little need for overarching control. Yet this creates the real potential for locking in lag and thereby promoting permanent inflexibility to change—making it more difficult to respond to uncertainty and change.

Tactical Lean: For Better or Worse

The first major challenge is advancing beyond *tactical lean*—an array of initiatives driven by the general rhetoric of "cutting the fat." These efforts are marked by widely ranging activities that address problem areas as they present themselves. Major challenges that businesses and institutions face with moving beyond this most basic level of lean maturity include the following:

- The tremendous pressure to immediately tackle "low-hanging fruit" drives organizations to focus on immediate problems rather than prioritize actions based on enterprise-wide objectives or needs.

■ Sequencing activities in a way that builds progressively increasing success can be difficult within real-world businesses whose vast complexity and scope present a myriad of potential starting points and challenges.

■ Efforts can suffer a serious loss of support if workers and managers see lean as a superficial fix rather than a means for addressing the more serious challenges that remain.

■ Proceeding in a way that locks in inflexibility can backfire by undermining dynamic stability.

As noted in Chapter 3, implementing lean tools as part of a tactical solution can actually represent a *step down* in the progression to maturity, creating unrecognized costs or new barriers to advancement that might far exceed the savings realized from waste reduction. Conversely, tactical initiatives can offer a critical means for building a baseline of stability from which further advancement can begin. However, it takes tremendous leadership to ensure that these interim solutions do not devolve into a long-term focus for lean activities.

Case Example: Mitigating Uncertainty Through Tactical Techniques

The Defense Logistics Agency obtains and delivers millions of widely ranging products, from spare parts to food, clothing, and medical supplies, to military customers around the world. These include a range of particularly critical "warstopper" items, whose demand can spike with little or no notice and whose delay could have a tangible impact on its military customers' mission.

Rather than simply stockpiling massive warehouses of finished inventories that might run out of shelf life or become obscure before they are needed, a team of engineers and specialists evaluates suppliers' value streams, isolating "choke points" where production flow is constricted. The agency bridges these gaps by working with suppliers to increase equipment capacity, pre-position critical materials or components, and offer technical assistance to enable the speedy production ramp-up to meet emergency needs.[2]

Earlier this decade, the agency realized that further advancing this effort would take developing the means for more broadly assessing millions of items it manages. It created the Worldwide Web Industrial Capabilities Assessment Program (WICAP), which includes a comprehensive taxonomy for identifying each of millions of unique items based on their underlying processing characteristics (what products they go into and the general capabilities needed for producing them). This provides a point of reference for further investigation in identifying common actions across groups of items—a "leaner" approach for more broadly mitigating the challenges its supplier base faces in preparing for uncertainty.[3]

For the Defense Logistics Agency, these actions represent an important step forward, slashing the need for billions of dollars of inventory by streamlining its suppliers' ability to quickly turn out critically needed items during times of crisis. Yet the real challenge comes in applying these tactical lessons to progress to the next levels of lean—leveraging this understanding of how to mitigate suppliers' challenges and combine items into product families as a means for shifting to a leaner way of operating across its broader business.

Steady-State Lean: A Common Plateau

Steady-state lean offers a starting point for increasing predictability of operations—a foundation for advancing through the hierarchy of lean capabilities as depicted in Figure 6-2. Perhaps the most famous example was Henry Ford's Model T production line. All evidence indicates that Ford's buildup of value, from raw materials through his assembly factories, flowed almost seamlessly, giving the appearance that "Ford's factory was really one vast machine with each production step tightly linked to the next."[4] The result was high quality and extraordinary efficiencies, which led his company to dominate the industry.

What is important, however, is for firms and institutions to recognize this as an *interim* level; they must maintain their focus on advancing to more advanced levels of maturity in order to avoid running into the same hurdle that Henry Ford faced.

Ford's genius was in creating an approach that thrived while demand for his Model T expanded, filling a growing customer need. However, while Ford's approach was tremendously effective when operating within its "special case" of largely predictable, growing demand, the company's fortunes precipitously declined when the conditions on which it depended later shifted.[5]

Businesses and institutions today will often need to overcome broader operational disruption in order to lean out assembly lines, fabrication shops, or other activities. A key step for accomplishing this is better synchronizing their production and inventory control system so that it can adequately accommodate current operating conditions. Some might apply information technology solutions to better track inventory across the supply chain, helping to dampen the *supply chain effect* (the chain reaction described in *Going Lean* as demand variation is amplified upstream in the supply chain). Doing so can create dramatic results. What these organizations must recognize, however, is that these measures alone will likely do little to create the dynamic dampening capabilities needed to sustain this stability when conditions shift.

Too often, early success leads to complacency. Businesses and institutions tend to focus on stabilizing operations around their initial advances, targeting continuous improvement opportunities to stretch gains even further. Many do not seem to recognize that what they have achieved represents only the tip of the iceberg; moreover, they fail to see that continued transformation is important to mitigating the chance that efforts will be derailed by the changing conditions that will affect them as they progress on their journey.

As Ford ultimately showed, it is not enough to create steady-state efficiencies; doing so without concurrently increasing flexibility across all forms of flow can lead to tremendous problems when conditions ultimately shift.[6]

Dynamic Lean: The Foundation for Lean Dynamics

Businesses and institutions that have fully embraced the principles of lean dynamics will likely recognize the need for attaining *dynamic lean*—leveraging lean tools and practices to create an ability to right themselves when things go wrong and maintain internal stability despite uncertain or shifting conditions. At the center of dynamic lean is a deliberate focus on addressing the dynamic challenges within the environment—from understanding and quantifying customers' changing needs, to better anticipating sudden shifts or crises, to adapting internal methods to promote a steady, efficient response when unforeseen circumstances do emerge.

An up-front dynamic value assessment—the first step within the cycle proposed in Figure 7-1—can establish the baseline understanding for embarking on this course. A key focus is to point out gaps in understanding, identify lag, and determine focal points to guide the transformation. As described in Chapter 6, this should follow a clear structure—first stabilizing operations before focusing attention on creating dynamic stability.

What should the emphasis be? Once stability is attained, efforts can shift from streamlining processes to reconsidering how production planners originally structured the way products and their components are created. Most likely, operations were structured to produce them in a manner that promotes economies of scale under the presumption of stable, predictable demand. A major focus, therefore, should be shifting instead to a product family orientation wherever possible, rather than focusing on improving the way existing processes operate.

Why make this change? As identified in Chapter 4, shifting to manage by product families can create a far-reaching result that could potentially impact many individual value streams that have yet to be mapped, making possible new solutions that otherwise might never have been envisioned.

Other focal points include progressively advancing supplier relationships to promote variation leveling (much as was described with Cessna in Chapter 3, and further described in *Going Lean*), speeding changeovers (discussed in Chapter 6), applying Total Productive

Maintenance measures to reduce disruption from equipment failures, implementing Six Sigma practices to drive down variation in key operations, and designing products and services to foster smooth flow (explained in Chapter 8). This list is not exhaustive; other focal points intended to mitigate the impact of variation with an emphasis on mitigating lag (each of its four forms) should be pursued, based on the results of the dynamic value assessment.

It is important to note that attaining dynamic lean is complicated, in that it takes moving forward simultaneously on multiple fronts, systematically introducing incremental shifts to advance flow to operations, decision making, and information, without breaking the synchronization that can cause disruption along the way. Applying the transformation cycle (depicted in Figure 7-1) offers a means to deal with this by emphasizing localized shifts that advance operational, organizational, and information flow, while creating the broad-based improvements necessary to advance transformational objectives.

Strategic Lean: Bridging Strategy and Execution

Staying competitive in today's increasingly complex, dynamic business environment means moving beyond a way of thinking that was built around an ideal of consistent, growing mass markets—a condition that no longer exists. Such a mindset has driven a wedge between two basic elements that must work in conjunction to create customer and corporate value: an ability to reach out to customers with new ideas and innovations and an operational efficiency for producing the quality and cost competitiveness that has long restricted innovation. *Strategic lean* focuses on bridging this gap, leveraging dynamic lean capabilities to bring these factors together and create new opportunities that otherwise would not be possible.

This is precisely what the Garrity Tool Company, a small, private manufacturing company located in Indianapolis, was able to do. During the 2008–2009 economic crisis, the company faced softening markets for some of its offerings (in particular, automotive and aerospace parts). By leveraging its core lean dynamics competencies it quickly shifted directions, increasing business in other, more stable markets, including the production of high-precision medical devices. In doing so, it was able to sustain a largely stable business base, overcoming serious challenges and strengthening its position to advance when business conditions improved.[7]

Pursuing new business strategies requires drawing on an increased understanding of customers' dynamic needs, in conjunction with leaner internal capabilities, to create steady, growing value across a broad range of circumstances. They must leverage the flexibility and responsiveness to change that come from developing dynamic lean capabilities, spring-boarding off of these strengths to overcome traditional resistance to change—in sharp contrast to companies that focus largely on opportunities within traditional market segments.

Caution: The Importance of Looking Outside the Business

Too often, lean initiatives focus on reducing internal wastes, presuming that this will somehow lead to increased customer value. Strategic lean instead focuses on prioritizing resources for incrementally advancing toward a clearer vision of value as defined by the customer. Before focusing on internal improvements, this means beginning by looking outside the business.

- **Start with the customer.** Many businesses and public institutions only generally understand who their customers are as they seek to gain a share of broad market segments. A *strategic lean* analysis should seek to gain specific insight into customers' changing needs and desires—with a focus on transforming the market.

- **Gain insight into the customers' challenges.** A dynamic analysis should begin by assessing how today's climate of change and uncertainty *impacts the business's customers*—making this the starting point for defining value.

- **Prepare for business uncertainty.** Business systems and capabilities are often implemented for *anticipated* conditions, setting up the organization for crisis and loss when the unexpected ultimately emerges. Scenario planning can provide a helpful starting point for incorporating flexible capabilities to mitigate unforeseen challenges.

- **Reach for collaborative business opportunities.** Creating personalized solutions that meet the customers' specific needs is a powerful way for leveraging dynamic operational capabilities for building customer loyalty and driving corporate success (described in Chapter 9).

- **Map the value curve** as a first step for identifying the extent of lag and its impact on responding flexibility to the breadth of business uncertainty and change.

Sustainable Lean: Creating Strong, Lasting Value

The ultimate objective for implementing lean dynamics is to attain *sustainable lean,* a condition marked by value curve excellence. Organizations that have reached this level succeeded in so deeply entrenching the principles of lean dynamics that their value curves—the hallmark of lean—remained virtually flat even in crisis (described in Appendix B). Perhaps more importantly, they succeed in driving a fundamental shift in how leaders view the creation of value for their customers—reaching out to transform the business environment and reshape customer expectations to better value their capabilities.

One difference seems to come from how they manage growth. Consider the example of Southwest Airlines, whose approach runs counter to that of American business culture in that it does not charge ahead to gain market share or seek growth at all costs. Instead, it adheres to a "highly disciplined, self-limited growth rate of 10 to 15 percent per year."[8] Its ability to see beyond traditional measures of business performance allowed Southwest Airlines to avoid the rapid expansion that caused great challenges to even well-known lean benchmarks (even Toyota fell prey to this temptation, to which the company attributed safety problems affecting many of its vehicles that came to light in 2010—a hazard that even mature lean firms can face, as was cautioned in *Going Lean*). Instead, Southwest's strong but cautious pace has marked its steady advancement; the company fully evaluates the impact on customer and corporate value before expanding to new markets, and in doing so sustains both corporate and customer value.

What particularly stands out is Southwest's focus on transforming the business environment, driving a fundamental shift in how value is perceived. The company is recognized even by its peers for creating a tremendous degree of trust with its customers, stating, "They simply trust Southwest to be the best value around."9 Southwest reaches beyond traditional market expectations; when it enters a new airport, it draws customers from other forms of transportation to substantially expand airline traffic (between 30 and 500 percent), which the U.S. Department of Transportation refers to as "the Southwest effect." In doing so, it consistently raises the bar for value across the industry, transforming customer expectations in a way that makes its own offerings the gold standard for others to follow.

Key Point: Drawing on a Range of Lean Capabilities Across All Levels of Maturity

It is only natural to try to associate certain lean tools and practices with specific levels of lean dynamics maturity. However, it is important to differentiate *lean dynamics maturity* from the *capabilities* that commonly apply to these levels. Organizations at various levels of maturity are not relegated to using only the tools and techniques that might be associated with a given capability level at any given time; a wide range of tools and practices can be applied simultaneously.

Consider, for instance, the approach for isolating and mitigating "choke points" in a value stream, described in the example of the Defense Logistics Agency's "warstopper" efforts in the Mitigating Uncertainty Through Tactical Techniques sidebar—a tactical approach for mitigating operational lag and reducing uncertainty and delay in obtaining specific supplies. A company might initially apply this as a way for attaining targeted improvements, essentially supporting its efforts within a tactical level of maturity. But as it advances to higher levels of maturity, these capabilities might continue to offer great value in addressing *families* of items; their resolution might therefore create an ability to broadly address similar challenges through these now-established product families. Pursuing these tactical actions, in effect, would help expand the reach of these product families' variation-leveling capabilities and thus support a much higher level of lean maturity.

What distinguishes a company's or an institution's level of lean dynamics maturity is not the specific actions it takes but the focus of these actions to progress through normal plateaus and advance to sustainable lean maturity.

8 Shattering the Barriers to Innovation

INNOVATION IS perhaps the least understood aspect of going lean, but arguably the most important. Many times it is confused with product development, which is clearly a core part of innovation. But innovation goes further; its essence is translating new ideas into a successful product or service, requiring an ability to identify opportunities and a willingness to take action.[1] And this is often where lean initiatives fall short.

Why is this? Creating innovation means breaking from the operations-focused mindset that marks so many business improvement initiatives. Innovation begins with developing a solid grasp of what the customer wants, along with a strong recognition of the implications across a broad range of interrelated disciplines, any of which might present constraints that must be overcome along the way. But most of all, it takes an openness to change—a constant willingness to interrupt the flow of activities whose waste has been successfully trimmed in favor of introducing something new and exciting that offers greater value to the customer.

But in some industries this creates a real challenge. Consider the reported shift in aerospace over recent years toward controlling escalating costs. Some managers now insist that new innovation must "buy its way onto the plane."[2] This raises a serious question. In an industry that has long been driven by advancements in technology, where is the benefit of promoting affordability if it comes at the cost of innovation?

Aerospace does not stand alone; other industries face similar challenges when it comes to turning innovation into practice. Health care, for instance, also faces escalating costs. Despite its many cutting-edge discoveries, implementation challenges have significantly impacted its success in making them widely available. One professional working within this industry shared with me the astonishing view that creating ways for delivering current innovations to the masses will produce far more benefits than all the discoveries in the next decade might bring.

Developing the ability to translate new discoveries into products or services is a serious challenge that must be met in order to satisfy the demands of today's dynamic business environment. Fortunately, lean dynamics offers a solution. By reaching across traditional boundaries to drive out sources of lag and by developing products in a way that supports capabilities that are critical to a lean way of operating, lean dynamics offers a structure and approach for breaking from this pattern and promoting new innovation as an integral part of creating value.

But doing so means adopting a very different mindset from many of today's lean initiatives, and taking a very different approach.

Leaning Product Development

Companies should proceed with caution when applying lean methods to innovation. They must recognize that this discipline is quite different from that of factory mechanics; applying lean, therefore, takes more than looking for physical waste along the path to generating ideas. The results of such a focus can be unpredictable and potentially undermine the core value their activities are intended to create.

Consider the example of 3M, a company widely recognized for its leadership in innovation. Early in this decade the company sought to apply GE's Six Sigma methods with the goal of lowering costs across its business. It appears to have resulted in substantial savings, but the company's reputation for innovation tumbled as well—from the top spot to number 7 on Boston Consulting Group's Most Innovative Companies list from 2004 to 2007, while the company's percentage of sales from new products dropped substantially (from one-third to one-quarter).[3]

This points to the need for caution. The process of innovation is substantially different from operational steps; it is thus risky to presume the direct applicability of waste reduction techniques that were developed for use in a factory environment. Leaning a company's activities cannot simply mean cutting the fat; it should mean more than mapping out development steps for the purpose of routing out excesses that do not create directly visible benefit to the customer. This incorrectly presumes a narrow focus in what these activities seek to achieve, and it trivializes the complexity inherent to these activities, particularly the many incremental nuances whose contributions along the way are critical but difficult to see.

This does not mean that lean principles do not apply, but that their application necessitates a different way of thinking. Rather than attempting to force-fit standardized tools and practices, those seeking improvement need to implement the lean techniques demonstrated to fit for this particular function.

What are these techniques? The first concerns streamlining the product development process itself—reducing variation within the process, bridging disconnects between the many design specialty areas, and creating the broader span of insight and shared responsibility that can identify and eliminate sources of disruption that rolling out new designs typically creates. The second has to do with overcoming the basic challenge of creating *a lean product design* that will actively promote the operational objectives of creating strong, steady value.

The Challenge of Streamlining Product Introduction

The most basic challenge businesses and institutions must overcome in their efforts to innovate is to minimize the disruption and loss that traditionally follow product introduction. Rolling out new products and services using the latest technology can force substantial changes to tooling and equipment, work procedures, and workforce skills. Factories must work through unforeseen problems causing workarounds and amplifying disruption across the business. All of this can have much the same impact as an economic downturn, with factories and suppliers forced to suffer loss until challenges are worked out and operations stabilize.

Complicating this is the disruption that results from the iterations that are inherent to product development. Consider the challenge of designing for complex products like jet aircraft. Teams of engineers that are organized according to their many specialized functions must design thousands of individual parts, optimizing the system as a whole while making trade-offs between a wide range of disparate performance considerations—like balancing requirements for airframe strength with the need to hold down structural weight. Further, they must consider production issues, reliability, and a host of other competing needs while working to minimize production costs.

Any changes that designers make in one area can have a dramatic effect across the entire design, requiring redesigns of individual elements and forcing them to reconcile the functionality of the whole system. The disruption this creates is most dramatic when design deficiencies remain unrecognized until late in the development program. This is a particular challenge where introducing late changes can create manufacturing challenges, disrupt schedules, and drive up costs, causing long-term consequences which can drag down customer and corporate value for years to come.

What is the answer? Improving coordination, concurrency, and integration of product development programs can be effective in minimizing these negative outcomes. The most prominent approach is a multidisciplined teaming structure driving greater collaboration and concurrency to speed the program while helping to optimize trade-offs. Fewer lessons will be left to be discovered at the outset of production, thus minimizing the startup pains or Band-Aid fixes that can have long-lasting impact. Yet these may not go far enough. Their project orientation tends to promote a focused mindset, rather than an overarching and ongoing shift back to the collaboration that worked well in the early days of aviation—an approach on which one Grumman executive fondly reflected.

> Part of my time I would be on the factory floor, working out detail problems with shop foreman Frank Baerst and the mechanics who were building the vehicles. . . . Engineers and factory people appreciated the importance of each other's problems and worked together for successful results.
>
> Peter Viemeister[4]

Streamlining product introduction takes a different way of managing the business as a whole—not just a way of restructuring its design teams. It takes more than focusing on the product functionality that meets the customer's needs; in today's dynamic, competitive environment, it requires introducing products quickly and affordably. This means emphasizing the traditionally lower-priority considerations for optimizing how they will be built. This emphasis can drive faster introduction, higher quality, lower costs, and greater adoption of innovation for greater customer value.

Designing for Lean Maturity

We saw in Chapter 4 that implementing lean dynamics means thinking beyond streamlining how activities progress today; instead, it takes understanding what is meant by value in greater detail and applying this knowledge toward transforming the way in which value is created. Product development offers a tremendous opportunity to go beyond how value creation is currently structured; it offers the chance to design products and services in a way that will best promote a lean way of doing business.

But where should designers begin? It makes sense to start as is recommended in Chapter 4, by gaining a deeper recognition of what lean efforts are ultimately intended to achieve. My study of aerospace supported this; it indicated that those applying the most advanced techniques for leaning their designs had made the greatest progress after gaining insights from leaning their factories. In retrospect, this makes perfect sense. Rather than pushing design activities toward some foggy destination, their more specific understanding of what these efforts would do for their factories enabled them to pull toward a clearer destination.⁵

Many companies, for instance, have come to recognize the need to address direct sources of waste, such as improving dimensional controls, which can prevent problems with fit-up between components that have a direct impact on product quality, reliability, and cost. But those companies that progressed further with lean production activities went beyond emphasizing configurations or characteristics important to support steady-state operations. Instead, they established configurations with features important to supporting their alignment by product families such as reducing setups—natural drivers for dampening disruption that could arise during product introduction or from other changes in operating conditions.

In some ways, this more advanced lean understanding seems to help reestablish a linkage broken long ago between product development and innovation functions, and the operations that build these products.

Key Point: Extending Design Benefits for Smoother Flow

Although lean design tools and techniques have become widely recognized and applied, their greatest strengths come from reaching beyond first-order benefits and applying them with a principle-based emphasis. Consider the following examples:

■ Reducing the number of parts is a well-recognized approach to driving down the time it takes to assemble the product, reducing production time. Moreover, decreasing the use of common items like fasteners, clips, and brackets can lower the number of items companies and suppliers must manage, minimizing inventories and reducing complexity. But a much greater impact is possible by seeking to more broadly slash the complexity of the bill of materials. Doing so shifts focus to reducing the number of sub-assemblies, unitizing components, simplifying details, and slashing the number of levels of buildup as well as the com-

plexity of production routings, information, and coordination. The result can be less lag and smoother flow—
improvements that are built in by design.

■ For decades, American manufacturers have recognized
the importance of designing products within the bounds
of existing process capabilities—establishing details on
parts that factory equipment can reliably produce can cut
production time and reduce defect rates. Some companies go farther, identifying key characteristics that can be
used in production as leading indicators of problems that
might affect consistency and quality. These can be used
to preclude failures that would cause disruption and increase cycle time variation—an important factor in translating gains to bottom-line improvements (as described in
Chapter 6).

■ Some businesses go beyond optimizing parts as individual
items, instead designing details using *group technologies* (a
design approach for maximizing commonalities between
parts, such as "materials, tooling, setup procedures, labor
skills, cycle time, and especially work flow or [process] routings"[6]). Applying this technique promotes greater efficiency in managing groups of items as product families,
creating the cost reduction and dynamic stability described
in Chapter 4 (depicted in Figure 4-1).

Innovation as an Ongoing Enterprise Focus

Former Procter & Gamble CEO A. G. Lafley noted that "innovation is
all about connections, so we get everyone we can involved." He explained that "the more connections, the more ideas; the more ideas,
the more solutions."[7] With lean dynamics, creating these connections
serves as the means for tackling complexity head-on. We saw in
Chapter 5 that mechanisms that break through normal divisions offer the means to expand individual insight and responsibility across
the business, enabling personnel to better identify and overcome the
key sources of lag that undermine the creation of value.

Very often, however, design programs operate against their own project-oriented goals, creating a design that meets predetermined cost, schedule, and performance requirements largely as a stand-alone initiative. As mentioned earlier in this chapter, even efforts to lean out product development tend to focus on design as a compartmentalized process. The best that such an approach can hope for is to speed up the development of a product that ultimately falls far short of achieving full potential.

Achieving a dramatically different result involves employing a fundamentally different methodology: integrating product development activities not only with each other but with all elements across the enterprise, to contribute to understanding and flowing customer value. Innovation must be advanced not as a separate entity, as is so often the case, but integrated into an overarching lean dynamics transformation. Although this creates tremendous complexity, employing the lean dynamics approach of decentralization can break it down into manageable elements while maximizing progress and maintaining stability.

Doing so should include better integrating innovation with execution and treating product design as an integral part of the solution to attaining new levels of capability.

Integrating Innovation with Execution

Competing in today's dynamic environment means continually shifting directions to meet changing business conditions and customer desires and demands. This requires an entirely different approach, a new mindset that enables innovation and operations to work hand in hand. Rather than competing with each other as opposing forces, they must work together to promote development of products that anticipate and capitalize on today's challenging marketplace. The payoff can be tremendous, but it requires making a shift to a new, leaner way of thinking about how business should be done and what customers really expect.[8]

How is this possible? In part, by extending the concept of *organizational flow* (described in Chapter 5) to innovation. Streamlining flow requires first recognizing sources of lag; this comes from creating a broader span of insight so that those seeking to identify improvements can better understand the implications of proposed actions. This is particularly important so that innovators can freely translate their ideas into practical, needed solutions. Its purpose should be twofold: maximizing the innovation that can be introduced and concurrently mitigating the risk involved in rolling it out.

Toyota, for instance, deliberately expands its engineers' capabilities to design products to fit seamlessly into its ongoing operations, a key to its ability. Before working as automobile designers, engineers spend time working in different departments to become familiar with the company's approach to business. They must do everything from building cars in a manufacturing plant, to selling cars through a dealership, to working through an improvement project to learn how to broadly evaluate potential solutions and seek out and coordinate with others.[9] The breadth of insight and collaboration skills developed are critical to maximizing commonalities between parts, simplifying routings, and reducing setups—characteristics that promote the company's broader ability to operate at an advanced state of lean capability.

Toyota caps this off with a Simultaneous Engineering approach in which it employs a range of methods, from including "simultaneous engineers" as part of functional teams (analogous to Southwest Airlines' boundary spanners, as described by Dr. Jody Hoffer Gittell in *The Southwest Airlines Way*), to creating more seamless interaction between product engineering and production engineering, to extending tools and techniques, so that all members within the design team can clearly see all aspects of the program.[10]

Lion Brothers, a leading manufacturer of apparel brand identification and decoration products headquartered outside Baltimore, sees the framework and mindset that lean thinking promotes as an important driver of innovation—a platform for developing innovation capabilities. The company has gone so far as to build an "innovation room" by combining several rooms at its headquarters facility. Walls have been transformed into floor-to-ceiling whiteboards; the room's only purpose is to foster innovative discussion that brings people together from across organizational lines to brainstorm new ideas for translating individual customers' desires into personalized products to enhance their experience.

Still, organizations must strike a balance between injecting new technology to keep products appealing and avoiding the risk of disrupting operations. Toyota's structured approach for rolling out technologies is described by James Morgan and Jeffrey Liker in their book *The Toyota Product Development System.*

> Each new technology must pass rigorous tests before it is deemed suitable for inclusion in a specific vehicle program. . . . Toyota creates a set of proven technologies that are "put on the shelf" until they are needed for specific vehicle programs.[11]

Seeing Product Design as an Integral Part of the Solution

Chapter 6 illustrated how businesses can advance in lean maturity by identifying core challenges and targeting activities to overcome them. Product design must act as an integral part of the solution, not only by creating designs that cause less disruption when they are introduced but by creating the means for value to flow more efficiently—a key to competing within today's global business environment.[12]

What, then, should those leading their business's or institution's innovation efforts do? First and most basic, they must maintain a solid understanding of the needs and desires of their customers and contribute to advancing new ideas and capabilities to satisfy them. To support this, they must gain a specific grasp of the challenges that must be overcome to make innovation possible. This includes recognizing the lag that limits their ability not only to roll out innovations but to create the value the company overall would like to create.

Finally, those individuals most familiar with the details and functionality of the company's products should actively engage with those involved in transforming the way business is done. By bringing their in-depth insights to activities ranging from identifying product families to rethinking production processes, designers can jump-start the types of activities that can rapidly advance their organization's lean maturity. Moreover, the insights they gain can help them identify new features and approaches that can further support these efforts in future design efforts.

Key Point: Considerations for Advancing Innovation

A core rationale for advancing in lean maturity is reducing the barriers for translating new discoveries into products or practice. Yet this presents a chicken-or-the-egg situation. On one hand, advanced lean dynamics methods are best applied to products designed with them in mind (such as parts specifically created for rapid setups in stamping or milling machines). On the other hand, the best results in "leaning" these designs are seen in companies that have already made substantial progress with advancing these efforts in their factories.[13] This points to some important considerations.

- The product innovation department should not be seen as an outside entity, but should be included from the outset in determining the direction of lean dynamics activities. Its involvement in performing the dynamic value assessment will not only bring critical insights regarding the intent of product configurations but will serve to expand designers' insights into the purpose, degree, and direction of the transformation, jump-starting their involvement.

- Advancing in lean maturity requires a tight integration between product and process innovation, each of which contributes to mitigating lag and its adverse outcomes to ongoing operations, as well as the introduction of innovation.

- The process of product innovation must be ongoing; it begins outside of the bounds of a formal development program with constant activities intended to promote increasing understanding of current capabilities, customers' needs, and opportunities for improvement.

- Innovation cannot be separated from the operational activities of the organization. While maintaining separate organizational elements has proven critical for companies like Toyota to sustain and grow the advanced capabilities they need within individual design specialties, it is critical to create mechanisms to promote a direct, seamless, ongoing relationship with the other elements across the organization.

The result is the ability to quickly and reliably create and roll out strong, steady value—a key to competing and expanding into new markets in even the most severe conditions.

9 Finding Opportunity in Crisis

S EPTEMBER 11, 2001, was the acid test for America's airlines. Without warning, the industry found itself at ground zero in a crisis that shook its very foundation. Demand plummeted, setting most organizations on a course to struggle or fail. But despite the severe challenges this created, Southwest Airlines continued to profit—even finding new opportunities to advance.

The real advantage came from Southwest's ability to sustain value across a broad range of operating conditions, a capability depicted by its flat value curve. With this, the company dodged a major challenge that undermined its peers, whose steep value curves made them ill-suited to operate within conditions that deviated even moderately beyond forecasts. The company quickly adjusted to the new environment, continuing to thrive even as others stumbled—a feat that seemed to defy conventional wisdom. While others were grounding their aircraft, Southwest Airlines kept virtually all of its planes in the air, rebalancing its routes and later adding new ones, including offering cross-country flights for the first time. And in subsequent years, while others were still shrinking, it continued purchasing planes and even hiring employees.

How was this possible? The company has a very different model for creating value. Southwest Airlines stands apart in that it is not built around the "hub-and-spoke system" that draws its efficiencies by maximizing economies of scale, an approach for optimizing internal efficiencies in predictable mass markets. Instead of fueling its need for scale, Southwest focuses on transporting its customers. In doing so, its results consistently defy conventional wisdom; the company is able to provide consistent, high-quality, low-cost service that quickly adjusts to its environment,

For Southwest and other benchmarks of lean dynamics, this very different approach seems to consistently open the doors for new opportunities—even transforming the marketplace to better suit the form of value it delivers. Yet, this is not a capability that can easily be added to a traditional approach; the means for creating dynamic customer value must be built in to its foundation.

A New Model for Creating Value

Much of the challenge in generating new opportunities from lean efforts stems from confusion as to what is meant by "creating value." Value begins with the customer, not with the needs or desires of the corporation. This means doing far more than reducing defects, streamlining operations, or even slashing costs; it means searching beyond the business to gain a deep understanding of what customers want and need. It means innovating products and services that meet the actual, anticipated, and even unrecognized demands of the marketplace—and quickly responding beyond what the competition can deliver.

Lean practitioners seem to understand that defining value must be the starting point for their efforts, but many lean efforts gloss over this step; instead, they focus on cutting waste under the general presumption that bottom-line value will somehow result. But this may not always be the case. For instance, what if a company's lean efforts succeed in more efficiently turning out something that customers no longer want? Moreover, what if the company succeeds in driving up efficiencies at the expense of innovation—the real value its customers might expect?

By creating a strong connection between what their customers seek and their ability to deliver it across their broad continuum of circumstances, companies and institutions can better adjust to their environment, even transforming customers' perceptions of value to match the form their lean systems are best suited to deliver. An important focus for achieving this is solidifying the interrelationship between the internal capabilities so critical to powering this approach and reaching out and embracing fresh new opportunities for creating corporate and customer value so critical for fueling success.

Growing in this understanding seems central to advancing in lean maturity. Organizations that plateau at lower maturity levels appear to focus on lean as an internal exercise, targeting tactical fixes or solutions based on today's understanding of their customers and environment. Advancing requires recognizing that more than simply cutting waste, speeding flow, and minimizing costs is needed. It takes gaining a deeper understanding of customers' challenges and needs, drawing on increasing lean capabilities for developing deeper and more innovative solutions.

Building Opportunities Through Customer Relationships

Connecting capabilities with opportunities at each phase along the way is integral to the process of going lean. Doing so, however, requires becoming more in tune with the customer than ever before. It means breaking from the mindset that customers all act the same, instead seeking to better understand their wants and needs. In other words, going lean requires reaching out and creating deeper customer relationships, increasing trust and even transforming their perceptions of value.

The first step is gaining a specific understanding of who the customers are and how well the corporation or institution has been able to serve them. As fundamental as that might seem, some organizations appear to be satisfied with only a coarse understanding of even their largest customers and rely almost solely on lagging, qualitative mechanisms (such as customer satisfaction surveys and word-of-mouth feedback during meetings) that seriously limit their insight and ability to take action.

Consider how much further Procter & Gamble, a company widely recognized for its innovative methods, takes this; rather than simply analyzing existing data on customers' stated or demonstrated needs, it seeks new ways for capturing customers' real needs.

> Great innovations come from understanding the customer's unmet needs and desires, both articulated and unarticulated—that is, not only what they say, but, more important, what they cannot articulate or do not want to say.[1]

P&G initiated a series of programs early in this decade to gain firsthand insights into the deeper factors that define who customers are and what drives their buying decisions and behaviors. "Living It," for example, immerses employees into the day-to-day world of their customers by actually having them live with customers in their homes for several days at a time. This program, along with a companion program in which employees work behind the counter at a retailer, has paid tremendous dividends, identifying neglected market niches and previously overlooked opportunities (like the Swiffer new-age mop), generating enormous profits.[2]

This approach is strikingly similar to the concept described in Chapter 8 in which Toyota's engineers begin their career by gaining a deeper understanding of what it means to create value, doing everything from building cars in a manufacturing plant to selling cars through a dealership before working as a product designer. The depth of the insight this gives them about the details of what their company produces and how customers perceive it goes far beyond traditional methods for understanding customers' desires and what it takes to create value for them.

Progressive advancement in their specific understanding of what real customer value means is critical to guiding how companies and institutions go about developing their lean dynamics capabilities. Rather than applying lean tools and techniques to reach toward a vaguely understood destination, their understanding and pursuit of specific opportunities along the way can create greater clarity and enthusiasm for its most powerful result: creating *customer solutions* that build trust and transform customers' perception of value. These organizations can progressively extend the types of opportunities they pursue as they continue to grow in lean maturity, advancing their complexity while broadening the depth and breadth of value they create.

Caution: Avoiding the Technology Trap

Businesses and institutions have come to recognize that building a relationship with their customers is critical to sustaining or growing the business; as a result, technology-driven solutions (most notably, Customer Relationship Management, or CRM), have become all the rage. But like many technology solutions, despite substantial expenditures, CRM often falls short of what it is intended to achieve.[3] Great care must therefore be taken to avoid the common traps that such solutions create.

■ **Attempting to bridge disconnects across operations or supply chains rather than eliminate them.** Companies must resist applying information technology as a means to reduce the challenges from lag that is imbedded in their current way of doing business—entrenching processes that have worked well enough when conditions are stable, but may stumble in the face of changing conditions, customer needs, and emerging opportunities.

■ **Guiding restructuring efforts based on technology capabilities.** A general hazard of implementing commercially available technology solutions is the need to structure the technology to support the business, rather than the other way around (which is how lean benchmarks like Toyota assess their application).[4] The effect can lock in current activities and structures that are riddled with lag, amplify its effects, and cut the company or institution off from creating the innovative solutions that are critical to sustaining or advancing the business.

■ **Emphasizing cost over value.** Even with technology, the right focus must be emphasized. A 2009 Harvard study debunked the popular belief that maintaining electronic records will by itself have a substantially positive effect on

> medical costs and quality of care. Not only did it show that the best of these systems did not meaningfully improve cost or quality but that they seem to promote more emphasis on the bureaucratic processes.[5]

Advancing Through Trust

What stands out the most about organizations that have moved to advanced stages of lean dynamics? Their ability to turn out solid, consistent value—a powerful means for engendering a deep sense of customer trust. Customers come back time and time again, in large part due to the consistency of what they offer; customers know they can depend on the business's high quality, great service, and fair price every time they return. And it is this deep sense of trust that is fundamental to creating new opportunities.

Think about how Walmart's "everyday low-prices," along with its broad range of products, overcomes the potential for customers to perceive its large, out-of-the way stores as inconvenient. Instead, people have come to see them as a destination. Furthermore, customers' trust in Walmart's prices helps to make the most of stores' already engaged shoppers, who trust that if they see something they want, they need not shop around.[6] The result is a powerful cycle of customer trust and loyalty:

> Customers will return again and again, and that is where the real profit in this business lies, not in trying to drag strangers into your stores for one-time purchases based on splashy sales or expensive advertising.[7]

Even competitors recognize the tremendous opportunity that comes from the deeply held customer trust that these companies create, which gives them a distinct competitive advantage. Jerry Grindstein, chief executive of Delta Air Lines, noted that customers were switching to Southwest Airlines because they did not trust that they were getting a good deal from others:

Southwest succeeded so well that today customers flock to the airline's
Web site, even when Southwest's prices are higher than other carriers'.
They simply trust Southwest to be the best value around.[8]

Trust is a key outcome of going lean. Organizations that gain the
ability to create consistent, strong value are able to form impeccable
reputations for excellence. This reputation is powerful, in that it creates the potential for greater customer loyalty, generating opportunities for sustaining business across a range of conditions—even for
attracting new business during the worst of times.

Consider the Garrity Tool Company, which produces complex
and often critical items, many of which are used in military aircraft
and medical systems. Like many small manufacturers, this company was initially struck by declining sales as part of the dramatic
downturn during the recession in 2008. What made this company
stand out was how quickly it was able to recover and pull in new
business to generate banner revenues long before the recession was
declared over.

How was this possible? As Don Garrity, the company's president, put it, "by creating new opportunities that draw on our lean
capabilities for quickly turning out what they need."[9] Don knows
what his customers need from him. His company has long stood out
because of its reputation for excellence; customers trust that his
business will quickly and reliably respond to even last-minute demands, turn out the highest-quality parts, meet the most stringent
requirements, and deliver them when the customer needs them. As
demand for aerospace parts dried up, he shifted his focus to medical
devices. The result was not simply greater revenues (2009 was the
high watermark in company sales—a 16 percent increase over its
previous record) but open doors for new business expansion into the
future.

Creating Customer-Driven Solutions

Establishing a solid reputation for excellence by rapidly responding to
customers' changing needs opens the doors for reaching beyond traditional ways of thinking about products and services. This can give

businesses the customer forum they require to understand these needs, including collaborating with clients to help them understand the art of the possible.[10]

Lion Brothers does just this; this lean producer of apparel brand identification and decoration products (logos that are recognized around the world) has begun collaborating with its customers to more precisely meet their needs, extending the art of the possible into areas that otherwise would have been considered unheard of. By leveraging its lean factories in conjunction with its rapid design capabilities and patented processes, Lion Brothers can create and produce substantial quantities of a specific product within days of finalizing the customer's design.

The company created a culture of "structured experimentation," drawing on its lean capabilities to reach across normal organizational lines and bring together the best ideas to create a range of solutions.

> As we experimented, we realized that we needed to experiment more. That led us to increase our research and development capabilities, which, in turn, led us to commercialize more—offer more products and services. Over time this led us to swap over from being simply a manufacturer to an innovations company.
>
> Susan Ganz, CEO of Lion Brothers[11]

Building trust with the customer and adopting a mindset of continuous advancement and innovation is what really makes lean dynamics come together as a powerful system for doing business. This means working with customers to transform their ways of thinking and create customer solutions, with benefits far beyond the tangible product the company delivers.

Marlin Wire, a Baltimore manufacturer of industrial-grade steel baskets, demonstrates another spin on this principle. Like other lean successes, the company began its journey out of the need to overcome serious challenges that confronted its business environment. When CEO Drew Greenblatt bought the Marlin Wire company in 1992, it was simply a bagel basket manufacturer—the largest in America. But, he explained, he had to change when Chinese manufacturers targeted his niche: "They could produce and deliver these baskets cheaper than I could get the material."[12] He quickly realized that thriving—or even surviving—would take an entirely different approach.

Like Lion Brothers, Marlin Wire goes beyond responding to customers' stated needs; it draws on its lean capabilities to innovate solutions that never before seemed possible. Central to its approach is collaboration with customers—working to increase their understanding of how the company's products can more effectively and completely address clients' real needs. As part of Marlin Wire's effort to design baskets used by manufacturers to store and transport parts, its engineers seek to improve their process efficiencies. Through data analysis, conferences with clients, and even site visits, they come up with better ways for handling parts, slashing the steps required for substantial improvement in operational flow.

For example, the company worked with a Toyota supplier of brake calipers to create an overall solution to precisely transport one "lot size" through its progression of fabrication steps, from machining to plating, cleaning, and assembly—eliminating the waste from managing parts individually as was previously necessary. Over time, such solutions can add up to huge savings (and reduced lag), making Marlin Wire's products seem like a real bargain.[13]

Speed and responsiveness—attributes of lean operations—are now fundamental to Marlin Wire's approach. Its ability to transform orders into designs and then deliver small and large quantities of products better and faster than competitors was key to landing substantial orders from new customers at the height of the recession. And it recently spun off its ability to rapidly design and fabricate fixtures that precisely position and hold wires for welding (an important contributor to its high quality and rapid production) into a new line of work—producing check fixtures for outside customers like Toyota, supporting their ability to manage lean operations.

Adopting such a mindset makes possible business relationships that can overcome some of the greatest challenges facing companies today. As customers feel more comfortable collaborating on solutions, they tend to overcome their sense of risk and become more confident in the possibility of stretching even further—perhaps opening the doors to innovative ways to address their deepest challenges.[14] Complexity can be transformed from a challenge to a competitive advantage. The results can be astounding, extending far beyond the narrow solutions driven by traditional management methods, reaching toward a new realm of possibilities.

Leveraging Downturns for Operational Gains

Many years ago, as a long distance runner I learned that it was difficult to break away from the pack on level ground. After spending time training on hills, I found that I was able to speed ahead during a race when others struggled against these conditions. This seems analogous to what lean dynamics organizations can do; challenging conditions that cause others to struggle can actually represent opportunities for breaking away from the pack.

Lean dynamics benchmarks clearly see the importance of sustaining or even growing operational capabilities when times are toughest. In 2008, when skyrocketing gasoline prices drove down demand for Toyota's large trucks, the company was forced to suspend production of some of these vehicles. But instead of laying off employees at its Tundra factory in San Antonio, Texas, it kept its workers on the payroll, scheduling them for training, work at other facilities, and even performing community service, like removing graffiti.[15] The company did this because of the need to retain its employees' skills and to keep from compromising their trust. Walmart has a history of hiring trained managers who become available as other companies struggling through downturns lay them off. And Southwest Airlines continued to grow after September 11, purchasing new planes, expanding to new routes, and picking up airport gates dropped by others.[16]

Marlin Wire shows that this works for small businesses as well. During my visit in late 2009, I watched as its factory speedily processed a new order for five thousand baskets, cutting, welding, forming, checking, and trimming a complex array of wire elements with little inventory and very short wait time between steps. "We exploit our speed," CEO Drew Greenblatt explained. As he put it, his company lands new clients because of its consistently high quality and tremendous responsiveness to even large, short-turnaround orders. "Our revenue grows because we're lean."[17]

During the 2008–2009 recession, Marlin Wire continued to improve its efficiencies, restructuring the way it did business to reduce
inventories in raw materials and finished goods. As Mr. Greenblatt
put it, "We found more than $300,000 in cash during a recession,"
simply by doing things better. And the company expanded, investing
in new equipment, hiring new employees, and increasing year-over-
year sales by 40 percent.[18, 19]

Cessna took yet another path. It used its reduced pace of operations (and that of its suppliers) during the recession as an opportunity to expand its lean efforts, reaching even deeper by applying new
applications of these principles in preparation for the next shift
in business conditions. In order to promote the efficiency of manufacturing cells (which it refers to as Centers of Excellence, or
COEs, as described in Chapter 4), it expanded the concept to
"process COEs," making agreements with plating or other processing shops, leveraging the same concept of aggregating demands to
slash lead times for performing these steps from weeks to only a
couple of days.

Moreover, the company began including low demand items like
spare parts in its COE arrangements. By leveraging its ability to quickly
shift to produce any item within its dedicated product family, its suppliers demonstrated the ability to slash lead times from as many as
eight months to just a couple of weeks. The result is an even broader
range of possibilities for products and services that go beyond producing new aircraft.[20]

Although these companies represent very different businesses
and face very different constraints, they demonstrate the tremendous
benefit of driving toward advanced lean dynamics capabilities even
during an extreme downturn. Each, in its own way, seems to be on
target for creating new opportunities to advance while others simply
hunker down and wait.

Fostering Dynamic Customer Solutions

Henry Ford's Model T offers a classic example of a product that became widely successful because it represented an innovative customer solution. His design stood out among hundreds of competitors'

because it represented a complete solution that satisfied the wide range of issues that drove customers' needs.

The Model T was well equipped for dealing with the array of challenges presented by displacing the horse and buggy. For instance, its structure was highly durable and repairable—critical features, since it would have to operate on rugged roads (mostly horse trails). Its repair was fairly straightforward, its design simple, as it was made up of interchangeable parts. Each of these characteristics was important because the Model T would need to be serviced primarily by the owner (there were no service stations at the time). And its functionality was adaptable; it could even be used to drive farm equipment—a duel usage that likely appealed to a broader base of consumers. Perhaps most important of all, Ford was able to produce it in a highly efficient manner that made it widely affordable to the masses.[21]

Where Henry Ford went wrong was that he did not seem to recognize that customers' perception of value is fleeting. He was not prepared to respond when customer interest eventually moved on—when evolving conditions, such as an increasingly saturated market for entry-level vehicles and GM's "mass-class" market, made it possible for consumers to trade up through product lines.

Many companies and institutions face the same challenge today. Too often, they get caught up looking in the rearview mirror, producing products and services for what customers were satisfied with yesterday, simply refining the strategies they previously created in very different times. Often, even their lean efforts do not help; by honing in on waste reduction without first identifying what constitutes value, they risk focusing on changes that succeed in cutting costs but do little to further their opportunities. In addition, they risk taking actions that lock in their unpreparedness to follow new opportunities—if they could learn to see them.

Instead, lean transformation efforts need to continually revalidate what businesses and institutions create, ensuring that they continue to turn out complete customer solutions—products and services that strike to the core of what customers want even as they continue to shift directions. Organizations must progressively advance their ability to seamlessly and efficiently respond to changes rather than relegate efforts to attaining cost reduction for a static set of offerings, as so many seem to do.

And in doing so, they must continually reevaluate what they do and why they do it, challenging not only their processing steps but their structure, and even their culture, rethinking their business down to the roots of its traditions.

10 Rethinking Tradition

XPERTS IN FIELDS ranging from fitness to finance often point out that it is difficult to achieve success if you cannot first visualize it in your mind. Establishing a clear picture of precisely what success looks like offers a powerful means for staying the course when things get difficult. Like a beacon on the horizon, this vision of success serves as a guide, pointing to the final destination at each point along the way.

How does this relate to going lean? In many ways, advancing in lean maturity presents similar challenges: The journey can be long (particularly for vast, complex businesses, as described at the beginning of this book); it requires discipline and constancy of purpose; and it is easy to get derailed along the way. In order to stay the course, companies and institutions must come to envision precisely where they stand and where they wish to go. They must come to clearly see the reasons for their shift, the steps along the way, and the reasons that stagnating before they attain true lean sustainability cannot be an option. Their dynamic value assessment can serve as a focal point, but, like so many aspects of lean, this is only a tool. Gaining a deeply entrenched understanding of what lean dynamics is all about is what they need.

Yet many businesses and institutions do not begin by creating and sustaining a clear vision of their end point. In fact, the approach that many choose for going lean can, instead, contribute to obscuring this understanding from the outset.

Choosing a Path

Some lean researchers and practitioners emphasize the importance of learning by doing—jumping in and getting started as quickly as possible—and in doing so learning firsthand the power of what this approach can accomplish. While this makes sense within smaller operations, it can cause problems within more expansive businesses.

How can this be a problem? The greater the operational scope, the more workers' span of insight tends to be compartmentalized. Proceeding without first restructuring to promote organizational flow, as described in Chapter 5, leaves people to come up with solutions based on a constrained perspective. As explained in *Going Lean*, this can prevent them from seeing the deeper lag and loss that their actions must overcome, causing them to simply "tamper" with a system they do not sufficiently understand.

Even worse, this leap to action can cause lean objectives to be trivialized. People come to see the application of lean tools and techniques as the focus of their actions, rather than setting their sights on achieving the deeper capabilities that these are intended to facilitate. This creates a mindset focused on waste reduction and marked by tool-centric approaches for gauging lean progress that can be difficult to overcome.

It stands to reason that conducting an up-front dynamic value assessment prior to embarking on any lean dynamics effort will go a long way toward preventing the emergence of such a damaging mindset. Chapter 2 explains that its results can make the critical points clear when introducing the concepts and objectives of lean to the workforce, identifying ways for structuring the broader spans of insight, responsibility, and authority so that individuals can better identify and act on the challenges they will face. Doing this before launching into a lean effort can help by developing the means for all across the business to envision how a lean dynamics solution will ultimately look.

Recognizing the Limits of Benchmarks

Fortunately, as we have seen in this book, there are many examples from a diverse range of industries from which to learn. Businesses and institutions, large and small, offer diversity of experience through both succeeding and stumbling; their efforts have uncovered key elements that help point the way to lean advancement. Yet following their lessons too closely can be misleading.

For instance, when I visit a small manufacturer that has progressed substantially in its journey to lean, it is hard not to become excited at what it has accomplished. The same can be said of learning about organizations that have long ago reached an advanced stage of maturity. The specific actions they take, their tools and practices, and their focus on problem solving for continually improving their methods are held up as the key to success for all. These businesses demonstrate powerful results, clearly demonstrating the wisdom of their methods.

Yet each of these solutions applies to their particular circumstances: their size and industry constraints, the focus of their business, and their progress in advancing toward lean maturity. The presumption that these are interchangeable, that strategies will apply equally to any corporation at each phase of implementation, tends to misdirect attention. Organizations might focus on tools and methods rather than on creating the outcomes that lead to sustainable excellence in the eyes of the customers and the stakeholders. This focus can become a powerful force that distracts from a clear vision of success.

Rather than attempting to directly apply the tools or activities at prominent benchmarks, businesses and institutions will likely find far greater success by structuring a program based on the underlying principles they demonstrate. Not only will this create a more compelling argument to those across the organizations whose understanding and enthusiasm is critical, but it will much more closely reflect the changing needs of the organization or institution as it progresses through the stages of maturity.

Staying the Course

The ultimate goal of a lean dynamics program should be attaining a flat value curve—creating sustainable value across a broad range of circumstances. But keeping this perspective along the way can be challenging; organizations can easily become distracted by the successes they achieve along the way and then lose sight of this larger goal. And this distraction can lead them to backslide when they ultimately face circumstances that their interim state of progress is not yet sufficient to sustain.

Even the widely accepted benchmark of lean seems to have been affected. During the 2008–2009 recession, Toyota suffered its first annual loss in seventy years. It is difficult to fault the company, since its industry was hit particularly hard (and the company's losses were far lower, and took a much smaller toll than those of many of its rivals). To Toyota's credit, it did stick largely with its no-layoff policy (maintaining its other characteristics relating to advance lean maturity), recognizing the critical need to sustain a workforce that had become its most valuable asset—and sustaining workers' trust in the company, critical to the company's success.[1] Still, it was surprising to see that Toyota did not respond as well as businesses like Southwest Airlines, whose value curve remained flat.

Toyota's performance seemed diminished in other ways, falling short of what many believed it might have demonstrated. Most noteworthy was how it was forced to recall millions of vehicles for safety issues—a real surprise for a company so advanced with lean. Toyota seems to have explained part of the cause: It became caught up in the race to become number one and deviated from its earlier strategy, shifting aim to growth and market share.[2] In doing so, the company deviated from other core lean dynamics principles; rather than preparing for whatever came its way, "our flexibility was only upward," explained Ray Tanguay, Toyota's executive vice president of North American production.[3] The result appears to have been a dramatic drop in customer trust—a critical loss for a lean organization.

In today's increasingly dynamic environment, it is easy to forget how vulnerable any business is. But Toyota's stumble makes clear that any firm can fall backward in lean maturity. Organizations must fight the temptation to drift from the pathway to sustainable lean, planning for the serious challenges that might occur. Establishing and maintaining this mindset will serve as a powerful force to keep companies marching ahead, advancing in lean maturity as a way to better overcome the uncertainty that likely lies ahead.

Seeing the Art of the Possible

If businesses and institutions are to genuinely succeed, they must come to terms with the reality that today's conditions are strikingly different from those that many were built to sustain. They must begin by accepting that creating a fundamentally different result requires the application of a fundamentally different approach. Entire industries must cease to cling to practices that worked well for the conditions of the past and let go of the presumption that existing methods can simply be tweaked, not fundamentally changed.

Going Lean provided specific examples of the challenges facing diverse manufacturing and service companies. It compared leading businesses head-to-head, assessing their value curves to identify the distinct differences between those that displayed the principles of lean dynamics and those that did not. From airlines, to retail, to automotive manufacturing, *Going Lean* showed how companies of various sizes and different constraints can thrive within today's increasingly dynamic conditions if they open their minds and accept this new way of doing business.

Today, the urgent need for change among organizations is only growing. Educational institutions, for instance, face serious problems, yet they do not seem to be able to see far enough past their deeply held traditions to begin the dramatic transformation that they so desperately need. Lag appears to be tremendous; institutions appear so deeply entrenched in their rigid organizational structures that they seem to find it difficult to envision how they might begin to change. Yet the growing need to respond to dynamic challenges, whose implications affect people and industries across the nation, means that higher education stands to reap tremendous gains from embracing lean dynamics.4

Health care is another industry in which a new vision is desperately needed. It is astounding how far some hospitals have progressed in attacking some of the basic problems that escalate costs and put patients at risk. With hundreds of thousands of people purportedly dying each year from preventable causes, including medical errors or infections during their hospital stays, and with medical mistakes now a leading cause of death, those making progress, like PRHI, deserve great praise.⁵ Yet it is equally astonishing to realize how few health-care organizations seem to have made these advances and how much more must be done.

Finally, think about America's manufacturers. Rapid changes in customer perceptions, combined with escalating fuel prices and increasingly global competition, have made competing based on past presumptions a losing proposition. In a business climate where competitors' labor costs mean that the playing field is far from level, operational improvements alone are no longer enough. Moreover, customers expect more; they want personalized solutions that can deliver exactly what they want, at the highest quality and the lowest cost. Those who can best meet this expectation are likely to become the dominant forces of the future.

Creating strong, sustainable value in this environment takes more than implementing tools and tactics. Leaders and executives, managers, and workers across corporations and institutions must recognize that the crisis is upon them and that the time has come for change. They must see that shifting away from tradition is not the risk; the real risk comes from clinging to a sinking boat under the delusion that the situation will somehow improve on its own.

Where, then, should organizations begin? We have seen throughout this book that advancement begins by learning to recognize the gaps in the traditional methods for managing processes but also that the solution does not directly follow the problem. Rather than directly addressing process problems, the first step is to rethink value—fundamentally restructuring what they do to better suit today's dynamic business environment. Conducting a dynamic value assessment and then identifying transformational focal points based on pressing customer and business needs, as described in Chapter 6, can point to specific, measurable, and actionable initiatives that will begin to create real transformation.

This is the vision that should guide lean efforts. By progressing down a pathway that increasingly extends individuals' insight and involvement, businesses and institutions can progressively address their real challenges, and those of their customers, within an integrated solution. Doing so can create astounding results and open the doors for additional ways and new opportunities for meeting the emerging needs of the future.

A Framework for Conducting the Dynamic Value Assessment

THE DYNAMIC VALUE ASSESSMENT is intended as a data-gathering and evaluation activity to help in implementing lean dynamics by gauging the effectiveness of creating value within the real challenges faced by complex businesses operating within an uncertain and changing environment. It can offer important insights that are critical to identifying the starting point, implementation structure, and measurement focus that will guide a lean dynamics program.

Why is this needed? We have seen throughout this book that the best solution does not necessarily follow the problem. For instance, when we map out the progression of activities involved in creating a cola can (described in Chapter 4), we can see that it follows a tremendously disconnected pathway, filled with delays, wasteful efforts like repeated palleting and warehousing, and substantial material scrap along the way. The intuitive answer is to restructure these processes (following well-documented lean methods) to streamline flow and eliminate waste. Such an approach tends to work well for simpler products and operating environments; the problem, however, is that this approach does not seem to scale up well—it can bring confusion, conflict, and the potential to stumble when applied to vast operations producing complex products or services.

Lean dynamics overcomes this challenge by structuring around a less-intuitive solution. Rather than adopting a generic "continuous improvement" mantra, attempting to directly address waste everywhere it is observed based on the intuitive belief that it will somehow lead to improved customer value, it focuses these efforts around deliberately identified *transformational focal points* (described in Chapter 6). Focusing on advancing these makes clearer how individual initiatives should be sequenced, their specific objectives, and how to apply classic lean methods for eliminating the lag that causes the waste that degrades their value. This also promotes the understanding that improvements will likely be incremental; that interim solutions will likely be necessary, requiring an iterative approach to advancement—essentially a *targeted continuous improvement program*—rather than making a direct leap to the final result.

As depicted in Figure 7-1, the dynamic value assessment serves as the foundation for an iterative cycle of advancement that identifies a progression of focal points (based on the firm's or institution's capabilities and degree of lean maturity, described in Chapter 6). Initial focal points should aim at attaining a baseline degree of operational stability; subsequent attention can go to fundamentally restructuring how increments of value are produced by combining them into product families at different points along their progression (described in Chapter 4). Each of these should seek to concurrently dampen out all forms of lag—operational, information, decision making (organization), and innovation—while decreasing variation and mitigating its disruptive effects on operations and transformation efforts.

Where, then, should a dynamic value assessment begin? First, it should *baseline the organization's dynamic value creation*. Companies and institutions should begin by taking a step back from their day-to-day activities and taking a fresh look at what they produce today, how well they accomplish this, and how well what they do meets their customers' needs. This assessment offers a powerful means for moving beyond a conceptual understanding of lean dynamics and learning how it specifically applies to individual businesses or institutions, building a specific understanding of how well the company or institution is positioned to create dynamic value over time (which can be graphically displayed using the *value curve*, whose construction is described in Appendix B).

Next is *determining the organization's starting point*—both the relative capabilities of its operations, and its overall stage of lean maturity. This requires more than measuring actions or even outcomes, each of which can be misleading in isolation. It requires identifying the company's or institution's level of stability—where it stands within the hierarchy of lean implementation described in Figure 7-2, a key to determining which focal points it is ready to pursue. It also should include an assessment of its general *state of lean maturity* (described in Chapter 7); this can help point to the general mindset that exists—a key foundation for creating the vision, case for change, and plan of action that can set the course to advancing to sustainable lean (the ultimate state of maturity represented by a flat value curve). This is perhaps the most critical step; what is most important is the organization's potential to continue to advance despite the pressures to stagnate and simply refine gains within a given level of maturity.

Finally, the information and analysis gained from a dynamic value assessment offer powerful insights to help in structuring the transformation, optimizing starting points for the greatest benefit and promoting a seamless progression through the levels to lean excellence.

The following sections describe each of these three elements: baselining dynamic value creation, determining the starting point, and structuring the transformation.

Baselining Dynamic Value Creation

Value is tangible and quantifiable. It can be measured against what customers are willing to pay for what a company or an institution produces, compared to what it costs to accomplish this. Each of these is strongly affected by the dynamics of its operating environment (which is displayed by the value curve, described in Appendix B) and the degree to which the organization is equipped to respond (which relates to its lean dynamics maturity).

Assessing the dynamics of value begins with determining the extent to which a business or an institution understands and actively considers the impact of the dynamic conditions outside of the business—the shifts in customer needs and desires, as well as overall business conditions. This understanding serves as the foundation for determining how well a company will perform when it faces the threats to the emerging opportunities that its dynamic operating environment creates.

Key outcomes will include an understanding of major wastes and lag in current operations, challenges in meeting specific customers' needs, and transformational focal points whose advancement can broadly affect these results.

Assessing the Product

Before charging ahead to scrutinize processing steps for waste reduction, businesses and institutions should take a step back and remind themselves of what value they create and reassess the way they have chosen to assemble this value. Asking product-oriented questions is particularly valuable in that it identifies a path to improvement that is far more actionable, such as:

Does the organization have a deliberate rationale for the way it creates value? For manufacturing companies, for instance, reconsidering how production planners originally structured these elements (most likely to support a presumption of steady-state operations) and then restructuring based on a lean dynamics philosophy stands to create far more benefit than will simply focusing on improving existing processes. Deciding how these distinct elements will be produced—whether they will be supplied as separate entities or combined as part of broader product families—sets the foundation for everything that follows (as described in Chapter 4).

Is there an accurate way of displaying the severable increments of value, their relative importance, and those giving the most trouble? Identifying these increments of value is an important starting point, one that should precede detailed activities aimed at realigning value streams or restructuring business processes.

But many businesses and institutions launch right into efforts aimed at eliminating waste where it is most evident, either skipping or minimizing this important step, potentially cutting themselves off from deeper transformation and from the more specific, tangible, actionable focus to which this can lead. For instance, doing so early can create the opportunity for managing these elements together as product families (described in Chapter 4), thereby mitigating lag in operations, information, decision making, and innovation

Understanding the Customer

A critical step in conducting a dynamic value assessment is performing an assessment of the customer. Many methods for gathering information are available, ranging from surveys, to brainstorming sessions, to focus groups. The intention of this book is not to present these in depth, but to briefly describe the types of information that might help characterize the challenge.

Who is the customer? It is surprising how difficult it can be to answer what seems such a straightforward question. On the surface, those asked might see the answer as common sense; they might simply name the business entity to which they ship, or the purchasing representative with whom their transaction is coordinated. But, on deeper questioning (akin to the 5 Whys), this initial answer might quickly break down as follows:

- **How should the customer be defined?** This might not be intuitively evident, since parts of the business might relate to different parts of the customer's organization—particularly for large organizations.
- **Who is giving you customer feedback?** If an individual is then identified, does he or she have sufficient span of insight to understand how well your products and services meet their genuine needs?
- **Who are your customers' customers? Who actually uses your products and services?** Is it a worker on a production line or a consumer at home?

Identifying precisely who the real customer is can be difficult, but it is a crucial step to assessing how well the business or institution is meeting customers' expectations, which is what creating value is all about.

What do these customers value? Customers' needs and desires will continue to change; a lean dynamics effort seeks to anticipate and respond to these changes with efficiency and innovation.

- **What are their stated and unstated needs and preferences?**
- **What challenges are customers currently facing?** Are business customers facing different issues than the end customer?
- **Do customers seem interested in collaborating to create solutions that meet their specific needs?**

Such insights are helpful to identifying and prioritizing transformational focal points, which can help optimize the benefits that lean dynamics efforts achieve up front for the corporation or institution and its customers.

Do your offerings coincide with what customers value? Very often, organizations have little insight into how well they are satisfying the needs of their customers. At a top level, the result is clear. Poor performance leads to lost sales, which translates to lower revenue. Customer satisfaction surveys can glean a little more information. However, these act as lagging indicators and rarely seem to isolate the actual factors that customers value. Asking a few simple questions *to specific customers* might help.

- **How well has the business or institution performed in meeting customers' needs?** Can product characteristics, quality, turnaround speed, on-time delivery, and other basic attributes be broken down to show performance for specific customers?
- **What indications exist of the customer's trust and loyalty (this is substantially different from a measure of customer**

satisfaction)? What operational limitations might be contributing to these results?

■ Has the organization focused on mitigating the customers' challenges?

■ Have customer relationships advanced as a result of performance?

■ How do these answers relate to internal assessments of the business's strengths, constraints, and lag? Are customer issues seen as separate from internal performance issues or are correlations and root causes identified?

Integrating customers' perceptions of business performance is important to gaining customer trust, which can create opportunities for expanding existing business and sets the stage for moving to a collaborative relationship (whose benefits are described in Chapter 9). Moreover, these insights can serve as a powerful starting point for identifying areas that might serve as focal points for transformation (as depicted in Figure A-I).

Quantifying the Dynamics of the Environment

Taking a hard look outside the business at the realities of the environment is a key part of understanding the customer. As described in Chapter 2, this is critical for breaking from the "presumption of stability" that holds so many businesses hostage.

Doing so takes asking hard questions about the range of challenges the business or institution is likely to face.

■ How likely is it that catastrophe will strike again (e.g., Katrina, September 11), and what might the impact on the business be?

■ How might external forces drive different customer demands (e.g., spiking fuel prices affecting car-buying patterns)?

■ What disruptions might interrupt the flow of resources on which you depend, such as energy, raw materials, or credit?

■ Will government regulation cause you to shift your business approach (e.g., health care, environmental issues)?

■ Will competitors create new, game-changing products that shift the direction of the industry?

Evaluating such questions might include conducting scenario-planning exercises to help those participating in the transformation understand that conditions are inherently *not* stable and that any solution must address this inevitability. This can reinforce the need to mitigate lag that can amplify the effects of a disruption, building the need for flexibility and responsiveness into the core of business strategies.

However, despite the best preparation, it is unlikely that anyone would have envisioned such disastrous situations as September 11 or the financial meltdown of 2008. Therefore, what is most powerful about this assessment might not be the specific actions that it drives; instead, the assessment leads to the general understanding that business must be structured in a way to respond when the unthinkable happens. This includes mitigating lag to reduce the amplification of external sources of disruption within the business, creating variation-leveling mechanisms (described in Chapter 4), and taking other strategic actions that can sustain demand even in times of crisis (described in Chapter 9).

Analyzing the Data

Next, firms and institutions need to build a comprehensive understanding of how these real and potential external forces stand to impact their business. This is a critical, but often neglected foundation for lean transformation. Calculating value margins and relating them to product changes and to internal activities offers the ability to create a baseline understanding of the firm's capability to turn out stable value across a range of conditions (its construction is described in Appendix B).

A steep value curve shows that a problem exists. However, this is only the starting point. What is important is digging deeper with probing questions aimed at understanding why (using the 5 Whys approach described in Chapter 4). Some of the lines of questioning are identified in Appendix B.

Determining the Starting Point

The dynamic value assessment serves as an important foundation for structuring a transformation to a lean dynamics way of doing business, both at the outset and, in a dynamic fashion, throughout its implementation. The information it captures is important to developing a vision, strategy, and plan of action that will lead the way to real transformation. But this takes finding a way to focus the effort and maximize the early, tangible benefits needed to sustain enthusiasm, within a deliberate structure that promotes long-term advancement.

Categorizing Findings

Categorizing these findings can help highlight a core distinction of lean dynamics—that progressing with improvement does not mean beginning at the end and working backward; it recognizes that problems or challenges are often rooted in other parts of the organization, and seeks to understand these and address them. This is key to identifying where an organization stands so that it can properly address its challenges from a holistic standpoint for optimal results.

Although information will probably need to be gathered by functional area (using a process marked by substantial iteration in order to understand the progression of challenges that cross traditional functional boundaries), a way of pulling together this information is needed to spot trends and support major findings. Categorizing findings by each of the four forms of flow (operational, organizational, information, and innovation—described in Chapter 1) can help pull together qualitative and quantitative findings to form conclusions regarding key areas ranging from capabilities to major challenges within activities, between activities, or across the organization.

Identifying Transformational Focal Points

One of the greatest challenges to implementing lean improvements within a complex business or institution is identifying a starting point for taking action. Chapter 6 describes how aerospace manufacturers stood out in how they knowingly or not implemented their lean practices in a manner that progressively addressed a core *transformational focus*—creating a baseline for stability before advancing to more recognizable lean practices. This same framework seems broadly applicable; by successively addressing the greatest drivers for mitigating uncertainty and disruption, a core challenge facing many businesses, organizations of all types can advance in a structured manner to first attain a baseline of stability, and then advance further to more progressive focal points. Figure A-1 depicts examples of potential focal points based on this hierarchy (a sampling based on research in the aerospace industry) for implementing long-term lean dynamics solutions (described in Chapter 6).

Figure A-1. Examples of Focal Points for Transformation[1]

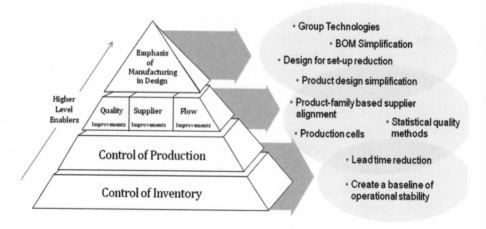

Managing the Shift

The results of the dynamic value assessment can help identify key focus areas within a logical structure that simplifies the complexity and scope of the transformation while creating dramatic improvements to customer value and promoting substantial shifts toward a coordinated objective.

A structured approach to lean dynamics will likely need to be iterative in nature, as described in Chapter 7. The dynamic value assessment should be an integral part of this progression, as depicted in Figure A-2. After identifying a starting point, restructuring to create the necessary operational flow (as described in Chapter 5), organi-

Figure A-2. Identifying Focal Points for Transformation

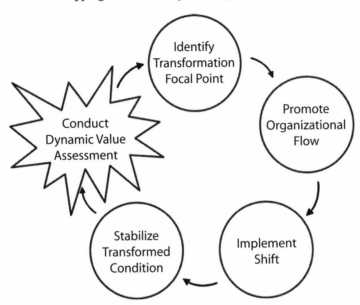

zations can implement the shift, and stabilize and measure results. Since carefully selected focal points will likely produce widespread changes crossing different parts of the organization, it is important to conduct a fresh dynamic value assessment to understand the full impact, and to determine whether adjustments should be made to existing efforts, or whether new objectives should be pursued.

Identifying the State of Lean Maturity

Chapter 7 describes how organizations tend to advance toward lean maturity and the general characteristics that apply to businesses and institutions at each stage of this journey. Why is this important? Because these characteristics can serve as a guide as organizations gauge their current state of maturity and lean dynamics capabilities, as well as point to where they should focus their efforts.

It is important to recognize that gauging maturity is not about simply quantifying progress in implementing operational lean tools and techniques; we have seen that this narrow focus can distract from deeper objectives, causing stagnation at plateaus along the way. What is most important is advancing toward robust value creation, as represented by a flatter value curve. Therefore, the key focus is on progressing against the four underlying supporting characteristics described throughout this book: *insight, inclusion, action,* and *integration.* Chapter 7 offers a number of indications that the assessment should examine, in order to develop a sense of progress in advancing from tactical lean to advanced maturity.

It is important to differentiate between assessing lean dynamics maturity and the capabilities that commonly apply to these levels. Organizations at various levels of maturity might apply any range of initiatives. An organization that has reached a strategic lean level of maturity, for instance, still might apply targeted, tactic-oriented tools, like addressing suppliers' long lead times by isolating and addressing bottlenecks using investments in equipment and raw materials to meet rapidly changing production needs.

What distinguishes a company's or an institution's level of maturity is not so much the specific tools or activities it applies but the focus of these actions toward advancing to sustainable lean—a key to progressing through the natural plateaus that can halt progress along the way.

APPENDIX

B Constructing the Value Curve

THE VALUE CURVE is deeply rooted in the very different way that Toyota looks at measuring its business. Taiichi Ohno, the architect of the Toyota Production System, disagreed with the way that traditional companies set the prices for their products.

> When we apply the cost principle *selling price = profit + actual cost*, we make the customer responsible for every cost. This principle has no place in today's competitive automobile industry. . . . The question is whether or not the product is of value to the buyer.[1]

Toyota shifts the equation around in a way that is mathematically equivalent but creates an entirely different meaning: *selling price – actual cost = profit*. The company recognizes that customers—not the company—assess the value of its products. And, like it or not, it is customer perception of value that forms the basis for pricing. Setting a sticker price higher than this will only drive customers to competitors' more reasonably priced products.

Profits, therefore, are not set by the company; they are simply the difference between what the customer is willing to pay (their perceived value) and what it takes the company to produce it. Toyota's approach is two pronged: increase the perceived value of the product and decrease the cost of turning it out.

But another key factor affects this result: the changing circumstances that impact both how the customer perceives the product's value and the company's ability to create it. In a downward economy, customers look at value differently; not only do they have less to spend, but they more closely scrutinize the benefit they get from their purchases. These same pressures might impact the corporations by driving them to produce at a rate below the point at which they operate efficiently.

This impact of uncertainty and changes on both components of value is depicted by the value curve. The shape of the curve offers powerful insights into the relationship between customers' perception of what the organization offers and its ability to turn it out across the range of conditions that mark today's business environment. A steep, U-shaped value curve points to an underlying structure that thrives amid stability but does not respond well when it is forced to shift too far from its intended condition. A company that has reached an advanced state of lean dynamics maturity exhibits a flat curve, demonstrating its ability to sustain value across a range of conditions.

The Elements of the Value Curve

The *value curve* is simply a graphic representation of the company's ability to generate bottom-line, tangible value as it responds to the broad range of dynamic conditions it must face. It is constructed by presenting the *proportional relationship* (not the raw data) between a business's two elements of value—value available and value required—on a graph to show how it changes across the range of conditions they face. The following is a description of the chart's major elements:

■ *Value available* is the tangible measure of customer value—how much a company gains through sales of its products and services to its customers. It is termed *value available* because this becomes the value that the company has available for all that it does. This is based on the company's net sales, a measure of what the customer pays for what it turns out.

■ *Value required* is the total cost of creating this value for the customer. It represents the portion of the value available that applies to all of the activities, expenditures, and even wastes in turning out products and services and selling them to the customer. It is based on the net sales minus the net income during a given timeframe (usually a fiscal year). It should only include costs related to normal business activities; it should exclude unrelated gains or expenditures, like those from large investments or revenues from selling major business units.

■ The horizontal axis represents a measure of the range of operating conditions across which these measures of value will be displayed. This usually measures sales volume and is selected based on the way value is delivered to the customer. For the automotive industry, unit sales volume can be used. For retail, this is depicted as sales per store; the measure for the airline industry is volume of passengers transported per flight (known as "load factor").

The value curve is intended to display the relationship between value available and value required across the company's range of operating conditions—not the absolute measures, which means that adjustments to these raw data must be made to make their proportional relationships clear.

Figure B-1. Raw Data for Value Curve Construction

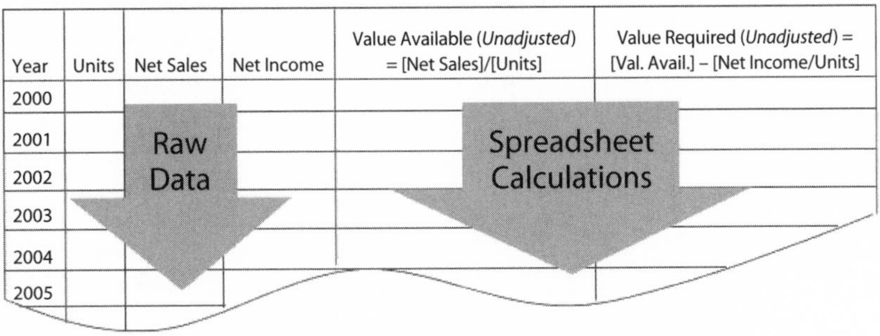

Year	Units	Net Sales	Net Income	Value Available (*Unadjusted*) = [Net Sales]/[Units]	Value Required (*Unadjusted*) = [Val. Avail.] – [Net Income/Units]
2000					
2001		Raw		Spreadsheet	
2002		Data		Calculations	
2003					
2004					
2005					

Performing Value Curve Calculations

The first step is to capture the basic information from a range of sequential years when the company's approach remains fairly consistent. It might have grown in size, for instance, but it is important that no major shift in approach (such as a corporate merger or a major shift in technology) occurred during the timeframe represented.

Capturing the basic data and performing value curve calculations is easiest on a spreadsheet. Begin by creating rows for each of the years that will be included in the assessment. Because assessing an organization's performance means pressing it to its limits, it is important to include data from successive years during which it is subjected to as much of the full range of conditions that might occur throughout its operation. Figure B-1 is a notional depiction of how a spreadsheet might be populated using data representing a company's performance during a sequence of years.

The value curve is intended to display the proportional relationship between value available and value required; therefore, it is depicted in a way that makes these proportional relationships clear—something that would be hard to visualize if we simply plotted raw data. The pattern that would result would be like that depicted in Figure B-2.

Instead, we can accomplish this by displaying them as a ratio, holding value required as a constant and displaying value available as a calculated proportion. For instance, the value available might be set as the maximum level for the range of years listed, identified as VA Ref. in Figure B-3; the proportional factor for each value added would then become PF = (VA Ref.)/VA. Each VA in Figure B-3 would have a different proportional factor (PF), which would be multiplied by the value required (VR) representing that year to result in the proportional value required (the final column in the spreadsheet notionally depicted by Figure B-3).

As shown here, the calculations involved in constructing a value curve are fairly straightforward. They involve simple arithmetic that can readily be calculated on a standard spreadsheet. However, much

Figure B-2. Value Available Versus Value Required[2]

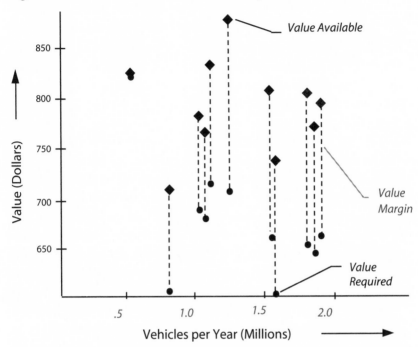

thought must be given to what the results represent. For instance, creating a value curve for a manufacturer that produces different variants of the same basic product or service is fairly simple (as in the case of an automotive producer in our example). It becomes much

Figure B-3. Spreadsheet Calculations for Plotting Value Curve

Year	Units	Value Available (VA)	Proportional Factor (PF)	Value Available = VA Ref.	Value Required = Value Required (*Unadjusted*) x PF
2000					
2001					
2002					
2003					
2004					
2005					

Spreadsheet Calculations

more difficult to determine how to portray value for a conglomerate that produces widely ranging products and services. In these cases, it might be better to break out parts of the business that turn out more consistent types of value, and map these separately. For simplicity, value required and value available can be calculated for a corporation as a whole (using net sales and net income) rather than applying the calculations by unit.

Another important element is the identification of the units of measure for the horizontal axis. For this example, the annual sales of vehicles serves as an excellent representation of the impact that changing conditions have on the business and represents how vehicles are sold to the customer (as individual units). As indicated earlier in this appendix, a powerful measure used for an airline's value curve is the passenger load factor. This data is widely available (it is a standard industry measure), and it represents how business conditions affect its unit of value delivery to the customer: how many people purchase a passenger flight. A measure used for a supermarket might be total sales per store, since this represents the impact of changing conditions at the point at which customers purchase what it offers.

Now the data can be plotted on a graph, as shown in Figure B-4 (note that the fifth column, which is constant, and sixth column are each plotted on the vertical axis, against the volume for that year, or the second column, on the horizontal axis). The example depicted in the figure is the same as that displayed in Figure 2-1 (early GM's performance from market peak to the Great Depression, whose calculations were originally depicted in *Going Lean*).

It is important to note that this approach depends on the ability to measure a stable system over time, and applies only for those time frames in which no major shift in approach is introduced. It then stands to reason that the shape of the curve-often the classic U-shape depicted in Figure B-4—is driven purely by the way that the company or institution responds to its environment. What comes next is to understand the causes for this—the sources of lag that cause the business or institution to respond so poorly when conditions extend beyond those for which it was designed.

Figure B-4. The Value Curve 3

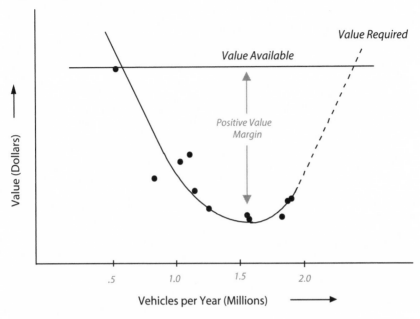

Interpreting the Value Curve

A key step is for businesses and institutions to build a comprehensive understanding of how these real and potential external forces stand to impact their business. This is a critical but often neglected foundation for lean transformation.

Potential Value Curve Indications

The value curve offers the ability to create a baseline understanding of the organization's capability to turn out stable value across a range of conditions. A steep value curve serves as an initial indication that a problem exists. However, the value curve is only a starting point; its real utility is in driving probing questions that support the dynamic value assessment outlined in Appendix A. Some areas of questions include the following:

- ■ **How responsive to changing conditions are the business's or institution's operations?** How well do the company's performance metrics correlate efficiency gains for internal processes to bottom-line results? Do they track responsiveness to dynamic conditions? Are the mechanisms for scheduling operations generally rigid and driven from the top down, causing workarounds when change suddenly strikes? How badly do shifts in customer demand or disruptions to the business environment drive shifts in how business is done?

■ **Does the business's or institution's organizational construct respond well to change?** Is it marked by a steep management hierarchy, leading to long decision cycles? Do decision-making roles shift during times of crisis? Are supplier arrangements strictly managed by outcome-based targets, or do they focus on creating dynamically stable capabilities? Do people within the organization have the span of insight to step in to help get things done when needed?

■ **Is information compartmentalized and complex?** Can people at different parts and levels within the organization clearly see how their activities and decisions support bottom-line outcomes? Are data broken down to support simple and meaningful metrics? Do these clearly relate to the creation of customer and corporate value (rather than lagging factors like inventory) at each station along the way?

■ **Is creating innovation a central part of doing business?** What mechanisms are in place to promote product and process innovations from all areas of the organization (including the supplier base) and to streamline their introduction into operations? How does the company or institution seek to advance the types of opportunities it pursues (described in Chapter 9), and how does this drive its advancement toward maturity?

■ **How well are lean capabilities integrated into the business strategy?** Are advancements in lean dynamics capabilities and maturity viewed by top executives as a central driver for expanding customer and corporate value? Is leveraging these improvements fundamental to the organization's vision and strategy?

The Value Curve as a Basis for Performance Measurement

It is important to recognize that the purpose of plotting the value curve is simply to show how the relationship between value available and value required varies across a range of circumstances—*what is important is not so much the curve, but the value margin.* Recognizing that attaining a strong, consistent value margin is really what lean dynamics is all about sets the stage for identifying metrics that meet the criteria identified in Chapter 6—in essence, to promote an expanded span of insight at all levels, and drive action that is consistent with the organization's short-term and long-term lean vision.

Relating value margins to individual activities and operating elements can therefore create a valuable linkage to desired bottom-line results. It offers potential to serve as an effective means for relating all that is going on across the business—from planning to actual performance, showing the real operational capability to respond to change. The result might be seen as analogous to Southwest Airlines' approach to keeping everyone across the business aware of the bottom-line impact of his or her work to creating value (described in *Going Lean*). This can serve as a tremendous enabler to driving down organizational lag, and creating a consistent, business-wide mindset toward attaining a level of sustainable lean.

Changeovers—Shifting equipment from performing one activity to another. In production, this means switching cutting tools, forming dies, and making other changes that typically require production to temporarily stop.

Cross-process metrics—Measurements that draw data from more than one formally defined process in order to relate activities to bottom-line creation of value.

Cycle time variation—The time it takes to complete the steps within a given activity or series of activities for one processing cycle. In a manufacturing environment, this generally refers to the time it takes to turn out one part, component, or product off the line.

Dynamic effect—Overreactions from the uncertainty caused by deviations from intended outcomes, causing a chain reaction across a factory and its suppliers that can be complex and widespread.

Dynamic flow—The progression of value-creating steps when pressed to operate across a broad range of business conditions.

Dynamic lean—A level of lean maturity at which companies or institutions focus on leveraging lean tools and practices to create an ability to right themselves when things go wrong, maintaining internal stability and, therefore, more consistent delivery of value, despite uncertain or shifting conditions.

Dynamic stability—The ability of operations to right themselves without the need for expediting or deviating from normal processes when subjected to external sources of disruption.

Dynamic value assessment—A concept used in implementing a lean dynamics solution; a systematic, holistic assessment of the business intended to gain fundamental insights into its overall effectiveness in responding to shifts in customer needs and desires, changes in business conditions, and the emerging opportunities and threats; identify sources of lag and transformational focal points, and help explain the shape of their value curves.

Enterprise Resource Planning (ERP)—An information system used to provide overarching structure and control of activities, intended to extend to all information and processes across a corporation.

Expediting—Reactive actions once a crisis emerges; creating workarounds to overcome disruption and achieve the organization's schedule goals.

Flow—The buildup of value as it progresses through the value stream. Smooth flow is indicated by the absence of defects, out-of-station work, and other delays and by low cycle time variation.

Increments of value—This can be an end product, an interim product (like a part of a component), or a major severable task within a larger operation. It is critical for lean efforts to stay focused on value rather than processes, which too often lock managers into a current-state mindset rather than driving a mindset of change.

Information flow—The movement of accurate, timely information to the right people at all levels and points across the value stream.

Innovation flow—The progression of improvements and new technologies into products and services.

Just-in-time (JIT)—A way of doing business in which items are produced and then delivered just when they are required and in only the quantities needed to support current demand. This approach differs from traditional factory or supply chain management, where items are produced in large batches and then issued from accumulated inventories.

Kaizen—A methodology used for fostering continuous improvement of activities, typically involving participants from the workforce.

Kanban—A methodology used by Toyota for fostering pull between workstations.

Lag—Disconnects within a company that cause its actions to amplify variation and increase its disruptive outcomes. Lag can come from a range of sources: from gaps between measurement and outcome, to discontinuities within flow of information, activities, or decisions.

Lean dynamics—A system of management, based on the principles and practices of lean manufacturing, proven to create strong, steady, tangible value for corporations and their customers across today's broad range of changing conditions. Lean dynamics is transformational; its principles and techniques let companies adapt to shifts in their environments to sustain effective operations, decision making, information, and innovation. And, unlike many other business improvement approaches, lean dynamics is measurable, offering a clear means for organizations of all types to track their progress toward achieving sustainable excellence.

Lean manufacturing—A way of maximizing business results by optimizing the buildup of customer value from its basic elements to customer delivery. A central focus is avoiding wasteful activities, delays, and inventories that consume resources but do not add to customer value. Its counterintuitive techniques of managing by product families (in which people, equipment, and processes work together to produce groups of common products or components from beginning to end) and building fewer items more frequently represent a distinct shift from the mass-production standard of producing identical items in large batches. The end result is turning out greater quality at higher speeds using less of everything, from factory space to labor hours and inventories.

Lead time—The total time from customer order to delivery of a product.

Loss—The adverse outcome of everything that can lead to lower bottom-line value.

Manufacturing cell—The grouping of people, equipment, and processes to produce complete end items, components, or clearly severable portions of major operations from beginning to end. They draw on the inherent commonality between items across a product family so that workers and equipment can quickly and seamlessly shift back and forth from producing one item and then to the next, combining work flow as if it were for only one item.

Material Requirements Planning (MRP)—An information system (computer software) used to provide overarching control of production schedules, inventory management, and planning activities within a factory. Often used as a module within a broader MRP II (Manufacturing Resources Planning) system that includes other modules for such activities as overall capacity planning.

Mixed production—Producing a group of items within a product family, drawing on their inherent commonality to quickly and seamlessly shift back and forth from producing one item and then to the next from beginning to end. This creates efficiencies even when producing lower quantities, eliminating the need to build in large batches and supporting the goals of production leveling and variation leveling.

Operational flow—The progression of those activities involved in transforming products or services from their basic elements to their finished state, delivered into the hands of the customer. This is the physical flow that we most often think of when we picture the buildup of value—and the most visible casualty when operating conditions shift.

Organizational flow—The timely progression of decision making by people at levels and points across the value stream to mitigate misdirection or lag. Smooth organizational flow is promoted by an organizational structure in which decision making remains consistent even when a company's "normal" conditions break down.

Process—A set of operations necessary to complete a major element of work.

Product family—A group of items that share significant commonalities, facilitating rapid changeovers that make it possible for manufacturing cells to quickly and seamlessly shift back and forth from producing one item to the next, combining work flow as if it were for only one item.

Production leveling (*heijunka*)—A technique for building fewer items more frequently (as opposed to the mass-production standard of infrequently producing large batches) so that individual production shops can progress at a pace similar to end-item consumption, thus offsetting an important form of lag.

Pull—Synchronizing activities engaged in creating value with actual customer demand at each step along the way—even as customers' demands continue to change (the converse of push).

Push—A way of synchronizing work using a top-down system for schedule control (*see* Material Requirements Planning).

Scientific management—A system introduced by the early twentieth-century industrial efficiency pioneer Frederick Taylor, based on the premise that careful identification and control of the individual tasks that make up each job can generate greater productivity.

Span of insight—The degree to which workers (and managers) understand the broader reasons for and impact of their actions and decisions. Organizations structured on division of labor tend to have narrow spans of insight, in which people respond to the outputs of other departments—often without understanding their cause.

Standard volume—An approach introduced by Alfred Sloan under which managers report their results based on their *average* production levels.

Statistical control limits—Statistically determined thresholds (upper and lower control limits) between which results are expected for operations not experiencing unusual circumstances.

Steady-state lean—A level of lean maturity marked by an end-to-end approach to addressing issues affecting the operational flow of a value stream. These efforts often begin in pursuit of whatever challenge presents itself first, with a primary emphasis on eliminating waste within current operating conditions.

Strategic lean—An advanced level of lean maturity in which companies have mastered dynamic lean principles and draw on the greater internal stability these create to pursue strategies for creating new opportunities.

Supply chain effect—A chain reaction in which unexpected changes in customer demand are amplified up the chain, growing in magnitude at each workstation or supplier farther from the source.

Sustainable lean—Companies that make it to this highest level of lean maturity advance at a strong but cautious pace—reshaping customer expectations and the demand of the marketplace based on their own capability to provide dependable value. These firms are marked by their strong, steady value margin across a wide range of conditions.

Tactical lean—An entry level of lean maturity marked by implementing an array of initiatives driven by the general rhetoric of "cutting the fat."

Taylorism—*See* Scientific Management.

Total Productive Maintenance (TPM)—A proactive approach to tracking and performing maintenance on equipment before its performance begins to degrade. It is intended to prevent sudden failures that can contribute to variation and uncertainty.

Transformational focal points—Critical focus areas around which specific objectives and actions are created to address major disconnects or significant hurdles to advancement. Their identification serves as a powerful opportunity to shatter traditional functional barriers—engaging people from across different functional elements to define specific actions and sequencing their implementation to increasingly expand their ability to turn out desired results.

Value—A product or service that satisfies a customer need or desire even as need changes over time.

Value available—A tangible measure of the *value* an organization's output represents as assessed by those who buy it. This is measured simply as the dollars its customer exchanged in return for a measure of output these activities produce; specifically, the net sales for the products or services it turns out during the measured time frame.

Value curve—A graphical means of portraying how much value a company creates at each point across the range of conditions that its activities must perform.

Value margin—The difference between value required and value available, when plotted against a volume measure, indicating how well a company's activities will sustain its competitive strength as conditions vary over time.

Value required—The sum-total *cost* of creating what the company produces for its customers during the measured time frame; this includes all of the activities, expenditures, and even wastes resulting from the company's execution in turning out this value. It is measured as net sales minus the net income for its output during the measured time frame, presented as a series of successive snapshots taken of normal activities over a period of time.

Value stream—The sequence of activities that work together to produce and deliver products and services ordered by the customer, from end to end, beginning with their most basic elements.

Variation—Deviations from intended objectives or outcomes that cause difficulty in forecasting and disruption in activities, driving a cycle of uncertainty, disruption, and loss.

Variation leveling—A less-recognized potential for dampening uncertainty made possible by the mixed-production technique. Rather than simply dampening the growth of *internal* disruption (production leveling), companies can use mixed production to dampen the effects of operating in an uncertain environment.

Waste—Activities, delays, or materials that consume resources but do not contribute value to the end result. Toyota identified the existence of seven common forms of waste, which it constantly seeks to eliminate.

Workarounds—The use of extra inventories, padded lead times, out-of-sequence work, and expediting that violates set work standards or procedures to overcome current schedule risks, delays, or disruptions within an organization.

Introduction

1. Paul Davidson, "Lean Manufacturing Helps Companies Survive Recession," *USA Today*, November 6, 2009, quotes Jeffrey Liker, best-selling author on lean methods, who states that "many manufacturers lose their lean-manufacturing gains after a few years because managers fail to monitor their viability as sales volumes or other conditions change."

2. James Womack, Daniel Jones, and Daniel Roos, *The Machine That Changed the World*, New York: Harper, 1991, 27–29, describes how Ford progressively advanced his system of high-volume, low-cost production, slashing assembly time from 514 to 2.3 minutes. Because he was able to manage for scale and stability, he was able to dramatically cut costs: "By the time Ford reached peak production volume of 2 million identical vehicles a year in the early 1920s, he had cut the real cost to the customer by an additional two-thirds."

3. In order to shift to produce the Model A, Ford had to discontinue his operations, opening the doors for competitors to take over the market. Alfred P. Sloan, Jr., *My Years with General Motors* (New York: Macfadden Books, Macfadden-Bartell Corporation, 1963, 1965), 162, discusses how "not many observers expected so catastrophic and almost whimsical a fall Mr. Ford chose to take in May 1927 when he shut down his great River Rouge plant completely and kept it shut down for nearly a year to retool."

4. Womack, Jones, and Roos, *The Machine That Changed the World*, 53–54, describes the labor settlement that set the stage for Toyota's new way of doing business.

Chapter 1

1. David M. Herszenhorn and Bill Vlasic, "Auto Executives Still Find Skeptics," *New York Times*, December 5, 2008, A1. The article quotes CEO Rick Wagoner as stating, "We're here today because we made mistakes, which we are learning from, and because some forces beyond our control have pushed us to the brink."

2. Alfred P. Sloan, Jr., *My Years with General Motors*, (New York: Mcfadden Books, Mcfadden-Bartell Corporation, 1963, 1965), 150, describes Sloan's innovation of the "mass-class market."

3. Ibid., 139.

4. This section's discussion of "standard volume" draws on the descriptions from Sloan, *My Years with General Motors*, 142–148.

5. This chart was first presented by Stephen A. Ruffa, *Going Lean: How the Best Companies Apply Lean Manufacturing Principles to Shatter Uncertainty, Drive Innovation, and Maximize Profits*, (New York: AMACOM, 2008), 36, but has been updated to include data up to 2008, further making the point that industry's operating environment is anything but predictable (this plot is intended to depict an overall trend and should be considered approximate).

6. Kiyoshi Suzaki, *The New Manufacturing Challenge: Techniques for Continuous Improvement* (New York: Free Press, 1987), 15, describes the seven forms of waste.

7. Peter M. Senge, *The Fifth Discipline: The Art & Practice of the Learning Organization* (New York: Doubleday, 1990), 89–91.

8. Jody Hoffer Gittell, *The Southwest Airlines Way: Using the Power of Relationships to Achieve High Performance* (New York: McGraw-Hill, 2003), 236–239. Gittell describes the airline industry's response to September 11, comparing this with Southwest Airlines' no-layoff approach (p. 242).

9. Herb Kelleher's quote can be found in Kevin Freiberg and Jackie Freiberg, *Nuts! Southwest Airlines' Crazy Recipe for Business and Personal Success* (New York: Broadway Books, 1996), 49.

10. These commonalities were first presented by this author in *Going Lean*, 65–76.

11. J. Welch and J. A. Byrne, *Jack: Straight from the Gut* (New York: Warner Books, 2001), 128.

Chapter 2

1. I am grateful to Susan Ganz and her team at Lion Brothers for the information they provided and access they granted for the description and insights on this company contained in this chapter.

2. Jeffrey K. Liker, *The Toyota Way: 14 Management Principles from the World's Greatest Manufacturer* (New York: McGraw-Hill, 2003), 150, explains the techniques of "5S" (which stands for *seiri, seiton, seiso, seiketsu,* and *shitsuke* in Japanese, or in English, sort, straighten, shine, standardize, and sustain), which today have become widely implemented as a beginning point for lean. A key problem is that, as Liker describes, companies can confuse this as being what lean production is all about; people rationalize that correcting the most visible challenges (such as creating structure, standardization, and cleanliness) is the best path to the result of reducing waste. But doing so can lead them to the same result as a company described by Liker's example: "We ended up right back where we started." This same hazard comes from most lean techniques; it is important to understand that seeing the problem is the starting point, but the solution does not necessarily follow the problem.

3. This chart was introduced by Stephen A. Ruffa, *Going Lean: How the Best Companies Apply Lean Manufacturing Principles to Shatter Uncertainty, Drive Innovation, and Maximize Profits* (New York: AMACOM, 2008), 49. The data to support this figure were derived from the table in Alfred P. Sloan, Jr., *My Years with General Motors* (New York: Mcfadden Books, Mcfadden-Bartell Corporation, 1963, 1965), 214–215.

4. This chart was introduced in Ruffa, *Going Lean,* 58. The supporting data were obtained from these companies' annual reports.

Chapter 3

1. I am grateful to Cessna Aircraft Company for the information it provided me to gain these insights. This background on how Cessna began its lean and Six Sigma journey was given during an interview with Mr. Tim Williams, Cessna's VP for Lean Six Sigma.

2. Cessna's business was hard hit during the 2008–2009 recession. However, even Toyota seems to have built its capabilities more for upside variation than such a sudden and dramatic drop in demand. As Ray Tanguay, Toyota's executive vice president of North American production, put it, "In the past our flexibility was only upward. . . . To

manage downward flexibility is obviously more challenging." This quote is contained in Alan Ohnsman, "Toyota May Cut US Payrolls as Unsold Autos Pile Up," Bloomberg.com, December 23, 2008.

3. Tim Williams, Cessna's VP for Six Sigma, made this statement and provided the insights on Cessna's lean effort in the preceding and subsequent paragraphs during an interview with this author.

4. This dichotomy in the aerospace industry was pointed out in Stephen A. Ruffa and Michael J. Perozziello, *Breaking the Cost Barrier: A Proven Approach to Managing and Implementing Lean Manufacturing* (New York: John Wiley & Sons, 2000); the scheduling challenge this causes is highlighted by this statement from Hectore Donald MacKinnon, Jr., *Aircraft Production Planning and Control* (New York/Chicago: Pittman, 1943), 55.

5. Brent Edmisten, Cessna's director of strategic sourcing and ISC strategies, made this statement and provided the information on Cessna's Center of Excellence program, describing its four-phase approach for deliberately planning its supply base: *Rationalize* the best suppliers, *align* long-term agreements to grow their support, *improve* performance by collaborating with them, and *integrate* suppliers as a key part of its business.

6. I am grateful to Brent Edmisten for providing the information in this paragraph.

7. Tim Williams, Cessna's VP for Six Sigma, provided this information.

8. This concern was identified to the author by Dr. Michael Galiazzo, president of the Regional Manufacturing Institute of Maryland, based on his observations during decades of work with higher-institutions of learning.

Chapter 4

1. Frederick Winslow Taylor, *The Principles of Scientific Management* (New York: W.W. Norton & Company, 1967, first copyrighted in 1911) is perhaps the best known source; his principles were published in *Shop Management: The Principles of Scientific Management* by the American Society of Mechanical Engineers in 1903.

2. A description of Starbucks' lean approach is contained in Julie Jargon, "Recession Forces Starbucks to Think 'Lean,'" *Wall Street Journal*, August 6, 2009.

3. Ibid., quotes a barista's concerns.

4. James P. Womack and Daniel T. Jones, *Lean Thinking: Banish Waste and Create Wealth in Your Corporation* (New York: Simon & Schuster, 1996), 38–44, describes the value stream of a cola can and presents this data on waste.

5. Stephen A. Ruffa and Michael J. Perozziello, *Breaking the Cost Barrier: A Proven Approach to Managing and Implementing Lean Manufacturing* (New York: John Wiley & Sons, 2000), 209, described that attempting to overcome visible waste in just a single step by eliminating inventories proved to be too much; a greater understanding of the underlying reasons for its existence was first needed.

6. Kiyoshi Suzaki, *The New Manufacturing Challenge: Techniques for Continuous Improvement* (New York: Free Press, 1987), 116, describes the "5 Whys." As Taiichi Ohno of Toyota comments, "If we ask 'why' five times, we may be able to capture the true cause of a problem."

7. Mike Rother, who coauthored with John Shook the book *Learning to See: Value Stream Mapping to Add Value and Eliminate Muda* (Cambridge, MA: The Lean Enterprise Institute, 1999), which introduced the concept of the value stream map, seems to support this with his statement in *Toyota Kata: Managing People for Improvement, Adaptiveness, and Superior Results* (New York: McGraw-Hill, 2010), 27: "A value stream map can reveal so many improvement potentials at so many places that it is hard to know what needs to be done. Attacking problems here and there in the value stream, rather than focusing on and improving specific process-level target conditions, dilutes our improvement capacity by scattering it piecemeal across the value stream."

8. Don Jones and Jim Womack, *Seeing the Whole* (Cambridge, MA: The Lean Enterprise Institute, 2002) describes this approach of narrowing down the span of focus for mapping value streams across different organizations within an extended value stream.

9. Rother and Shook, *Learning to See*, state in the introduction that value stream mapping is intended to help people learn to see the problem. The point made in this paragraph is that, while this is a critical goal, more is needed to create solutions, particularly within complex environments, where the best starting point for such an analysis is not intuitive.

10. This was a key finding documented in this study of aerospace manufacturing in *The Manufacturing Affordability Development Program: A Structured Approach to Rapidly Improved Affordability*, Final Report, Washington, DC: The Naval Air Systems Command and The Joint

Strike Fighter Program Office, July 1996. Firms that did not maintain accurate BOMs were among those that did not realize the most significant savings even when they had substantially reduced visible waste.

11. This figure was introduced in *Going Lean*.

12. Richard Schonberger, *World Class Manufacturing* (New York: Free Press, 1986), 111, provides this description of characteristics that support grouping into product families (and therefore manufacturing cells).

13. Ruffa and Perozziello, *Breaking the Cost Barrier*, 153–154, identifies how variation smoothing effect can be calculated, showing substantial gains with just a handful of items.

14. I am grateful to DLA for providing this background on these efforts.

15. DLA indicated that the results of follow-on efforts were mixed.

16. DLA provided the author with an update on this project, pointing out that initial results were "not duplicated on the subsequent phases of the project that included sheet metal and machine parts. In these cases the vendor's response did not show significant improvements. The scalability of this approach was affected by the vendor's internal champion and the vendor's ability to manage sub-tier suppliers to align their operations to the part family manufacturing processes." However, firms like Cessna apply what appear to be similar aggregation methods to attain benefits much like DLA's initial results, demonstrating its broad applicability to an ever-increasing range of businesses.

17. Thanks go to Cessna for providing this description and information on the powerful results that this approach has had in promoting substantial gains within its Supply Chain Integration activities.

Chapter 5

1. Alfred P. Sloan, Jr., *My Years with General Motors* (New York: Mcfadden Books, Mcfadden-Bartell Corporation, 1963, 1965), 138, makes this statement. It further explains that his structure did not support varying production to meet changing demands, a core tenet of lean production: "Such a practice would have reduced the risk of obsolescence and the cost of storing finished products for both dealer and manufacturer. On the other hand, absolutely level production—or the nearest to it that could be attained—was ideal from the standpoint of efficient utilization of plant and labor."

2. Stephen A. Ruffa, *Going Lean: How the Best Companies Apply Lean Manufacturing Principles to Shatter Uncertainty, Drive Innovation, and*

Maximize Profits (New York: AMACOM, 2008), 104–107, describes the
need to address lag to mitigate the *supply chain effect*—a key source of
operational disruption—which can be amplified by implementing
supplier agreements. Josh Cable, "What You Can't See *Can* Hurt You,"
Industry Week, December 16, 2009, describes how these risks were
becoming real during the 2008–2009 recession.

3. Jody Hoffer Gittell, *The Southwest Airlines Way: Using the Power of
    Relationships to Achieve High Performance* (New York: McGraw-Hill,
    2003), 31–33, contains this description of a discussion with Southwest
    employees.

4. L. Kohn, J. Corrigan, and M. Donaldson, *To Err Is Human: Building
    a Safer Health System* (Washington, DC: Institute of Medicine,
    National Academy Press, 2000), 1, states that "total national
    costs . . . of preventable adverse effects (medical errors resulting in
    injury) are estimated to be between $17 billion and $29 billion" and
    provides data on the number of deaths per year as compared to mo-
    tor vehicle accidents, AIDS, and breast cancer.

5. Dr. Karen Wolk Feinstein, president and CEO of the Pittsburgh Re-
    gional Health Initiative (PRHI), described this focus on "a clinical
    objective" in an interview with the author. Naida Grunden, *The Pitts-
    burgh Way to Efficient Healthcare* (Boca Raton, FL: CRC Press, 2008)
    documents these improvements, stating that "the work against infec-
    tion that PRHI helped develop at the WPAHS was recently adopted
    nationwide."

6. Dr. Karen Wolk Feinstein made this statement in an interview with
    the author and described the cross-organizational challenges covered
    in subsequent paragraphs.

7. This information is contained in "Pharmacy Agents for Change:
    Wrong Medication, Bad Chemistry," *Roots*, Pittsburgh, PA: Jewish
    Healthcare Foundation, 2009.

8. Mike Rother and John Shook, *Learning to See: Value Stream Mapping
    to Add Value and Eliminate Muda* (Cambridge, MA: Lean Enterprise
    Institute, 1999), describe in the introduction this third major form of
    flow: "Toyota people learn about three flows in manufacturing: the
    flows of material, information, and people/process." The flow of
    people/process is what this concept of operational flow represents,
    which this book shows is a critical enabler for fostering the other
    forms of flow.

9. Shigeo Shingo, *A Study of the Toyota Production System from an Indus-
    trial Engineering Standpoint* (Portland, OR: Productivity Press, 1989),
    155, states, "'The flow of people,' however, is entirely independent of

machines and need not adhere to the product flow." He further states, "The system requires each worker to learn the operations performed at the two processes adjacent to her own."

10. Robert Slater, *Jack Welch and the GE Way: Management Insights and Leadership Secrets of the Legendary CEO* (New York: McGraw-Hill), 233.

11. Peter Senge, *The Fifth Discipline: The Art & Practice of The Learning Organization* (New York: Doubleday, 1990), 23.

12. Stephen A. Ruffa and Michael J. Perozziello, *Breaking the Cost Barrier: A Proven Approach to Managing and Implementing Lean Manufacturing* (New York: John Wiley & Sons, 2000), 120–121.

Chapter 6

1. The Shingo Prize, named in honor of Dr. Shigeo Shingo, is administered by the Jon M. Huntsman School of Business at Utah State University.

2. For instance, Kiyoshi Suzaki, *The New Manufacturing Challenge: Techniques for Continuous Improvement* (New York: Free Press, 1987), 34, describes how Toyota divides setups into *internal* and *external* setups (those done when operations are stopped, and those that can occur even when the equipment is running), an approach that is not very different from how Southwest Airlines manages its fast gate turnarounds. While seemingly a simple solution, it requires substantial innovation in working out the details.

3. James Womack, Daniel Jones, and Daniel Roos, in *The Machine That Changed the World*, New York: Harper, 1991, 53, states, "By the late 1950's, [Toyota] had reduced the time required to change dies from a day to an astonishing three minutes and eliminated the need for die-change specialists."

4. This was a key finding documented in this study of aerospace manufacturing in *The Manufacturing Affordability Development Program: A Structured Approach to Rapidly Improved Affordability*, Final Report, Washington, DC: The Naval Air Systems Command and The Joint Strike Fighter Program Office, July 1996.

5. This chart was first depicted in *The Manufacturing Affordability Development Program*.

6. I am pleased to see that today, nearly a decade after my coauthor and I described this phenomenon in our Shingo Prize–winning book, *Breaking the Cost Barrier*, it seems to be catching on in the broader lean movement. Mike Rother, *Toyota Kata: Managing People for*

Improvement, Adaptiveness, and Superior Results (New York: McGraw-Hill, 2009), 80–82, for instance, described the need for lean practitioners to focus attention on tracking and mitigating the degree of fluctuation from cycle to cycle in a process (what amounts to the cycle time variation), a serious condition that is common and damaging, creating the tremendous uncertainty and disruption that, for many corporations, are at the root of much of their waste.

7. This was a key finding documented in this study of aerospace manufacturing in *The Manufacturing Affordability Development Program*.

8. This chart was first depicted in *The Manufacturing Affordability Development Program*.

9. Suzaki, *The New Manufacturing Challenge*, 237, describes that as part of getting started, firms might want to reconsider "the structure of a company's organization in the future so that job responsibility, information linkages, and reporting relationships will not hamper its progress."

Chapter 7

1. Mike Rother, *Toyota Kata: Managing People for Improvement, Adaptiveness, and Superior Results* (New York: McGraw-Hill, 2009), 75, describes Toyota's application of an iterative cycle for improvement. This, however, is applied within its system marked by lean maturity; a similar but transformational approach is needed for firms less advanced in their applications. The iterative cycle identified in Figure 7-1 is envisioned to support this intent.

2. I am grateful to the Defense Logistics Agency for providing this background on these efforts.

3. The U.S. General Accountability Office praised key attributes of the WICAP system in *Defense Inventory: Improved Industrial Base Assessments for Army War Reserve Spares Could Save Money* (The United States General Accountability Office, GAO-02-650, July 2002), 9.

4. Womack, Jones, and Roos, in *The Machine That Changed the World*, 36, make this statement.

5. James P. Womack and Daniel T. Jones, *Lean Thinking: Banish Waste and Create Wealth in Your Corporation* (New York: Simon & Schuster, 1996), 22–23, describes Ford's example as a "special case" condition.

6. This was also proven by the *Manufacturing Affordability Development Program: A Structured Approach to Rapidly Improved Affordability*,

Final Report, Washington, DC: The Naval Air Systems Command and The Joint Strike Fighter Program Office, July 1996, showing for the aerospace industry that even substantial waste reduction did not necessarily translate to the expected degree of bottom-line savings.

7. I am grateful to Don Garrity, president of Garrity Tool Company, for providing this information during an interview.

8. Jody Hoffer Gittell, *The Southwest Airlines Way: Using the Power of Relationships to Achieve High Performance* (New York: McGraw-Hill, 2003), 233, makes this statement. Despite these limitations, the author explains that the company has faced significant challenges in recruiting personnel to support its rapidly growing needs at stations like Baltimore. The trust and sense of ownership it has created over time with its staff seems to have been critical to carrying the company through its more difficult challenges.

9. This statement by Jerry Grinstein, chief executive of Delta Air Lines, is contained in Bill Brubaker, "Low-Fare and Hoping: Delta's Pricing Move Simplifies Rates but Leads Carriers in a Risky Direction," *Washington Post* (January 9, 2005): F1, F8. Gittell, in *The Southwest Airlines Way*, 7, discusses the effect Southwest's pricing has on creating passenger volume.

Chapter 8

1. A. G. Lafley and Ram Charan, *The Game Changer: How You Can Drive Revenue and Profit Growth with Innovation* (New York: Crown Business, 2008). A. G. Lafley, the former CEO of Procter & Gamble, distinguished innovation from inventions, defining innovation as "the conversion of a new idea into revenues and profits." He and his coauthor further conveyed the enormity of the challenge of creating new products, which goes far beyond what most people likely understand.

2. Michael L. Dertouzos, Richard K. Lester, and Robert M. Solow, *Made in America: Regaining the Productive Edge* (Cambridge, MA: MIT Press, 1989), 121, describes the aerospace approach of introducing new technology as "buy its way onto the plane."

3. Brian Hindle, "At 3M, a Struggle Between Efficiency and Creativity," *Business Week* (June 11, 2007), provides this information.

4. Peter Viemeister, *Start All Over: An American Experience: People, Places, and Lessons Learned* (Bedford, VA: Hamilton's, 1995), 187.

5. Stephen A. Ruffa and Michael J. Perozziello, *Breaking the Cost Barrier: A Proven Approach to Managing and Implementing Lean Manufacturing* (New York: John Wiley & Sons, 2000), 176–180, describes this

phenomenon and provides examples of advances in lean design capabilities.

6. Richard Schonberger, *World Class Manufacturing* (New York: Free Press, 1986), 111, presents this characterization of product family composition.

7. A. G. Lafley and Ram Charan, *The Game Changer*, 5, makes this statement.

8. Ibid., The authors state: "Innovation enables expansion into new categories, allows us to refine businesses considered mature and transform them into profitable lines."

9. James M. Morgan and Jeffrey K. Liker, *The Toyota Product Development System: Integrating People, Process, and Technology* (New York: Productivity Press, 2006), 168–172, describes the training and development required for Toyota engineers, for which focusing on manufacturing the product is central to the culture.

10. Morgan and Liker, *The Toyota Product Development System*, 153, 154, describes Toyota's application of Simultaneous Engineering (or SE) and the reasons for it and describes the *Obeya* and other methods to increase collaboration among designers, even employing IT for the first time to better share information among the team. The intent was to optimize labor utilization to compete with the low rates in China (p. 155). Jody Hoffer Gittell, *The Southwest Airlines Way: Using the Power of Relationships to Achieve High Performance* (New York: McGraw-Hill, 2003), 132–136, describes Southwest Airlines' similar approach of using "boundary spanners" and provides examples of how its operations agents perform in this manner.

11. Morgan and Liker, *The Toyota Product Development System*, 45, makes this statement.

12. Ibid., 155, states that "Toyota wanted to improve its manufacturing efficiency to a level that would allow the company to compete with the low labor rates in China. Company leaders recognized less labor in manufacturing depended on products designed to optimize labor utilization."

13. This was a key finding documented in this study of aerospace manufacturing in *The Manufacturing Affordability Development Program: A Structured Approach to Rapidly Improved Affordability*, Final Report, Washington, DC: The Naval Air Systems Command and The Joint Strike Fighter Program Office, July 1996. It describes that contrary to common belief, leaning the factory should precede major efforts for leaning product development because it points the way to creating leaner designs.

Chapter 9

1.   A. G. Lafley and Ram Charan, *The Game Changer: How You Can Drive Revenue and Profit Growth with Innovation* (New York: Crown Business, 2008), 45, makes this statement. While P&G's wide product mix makes it difficult to map its value curve at a corporate level (product-level assessment would be more revealing), it displays many of the characteristics of the advanced levels of lean maturity.

2.   Ibid., 38, describes the "Living It" program, as well as an example of a lost market segment that was discovered and filled through its efforts. Page 48 describes this in more detail, along with the companion "Working It" program, which offers a similar immersion opportunity from working at a small retailer. Roger O. Crockett, "Lafley Leaves Big Shoes to Fill at P&G," *Business Week*, June 8, 2009, describes Lafley's shift from innovating as an internal process to one of collaborations even with other companies. It identifies the Swiffer as an innovation that came from its efforts of learning by going to customers' homes.

3.   Eric Almquist, David Bovet, and Carla J. Heaton, *Collaborative Customer Relationship Management: Taking CRM to the Next Level* (New York: Springer-Verlag, 2004), 8, provides survey results showing that only 16 percent report that CRM exceeded their expectations, and 41 percent say that it fell short. It continues (p. 12) to state that getting a "360 degree view" of the customer "is limited by static, often outdated information about current customers gathered through current touch points, and fails to illuminate the value of prospective customers and changing market dynamics."

4.   Jeffrey K. Liker, *The Toyota Way: 14 Management Principles from the World's Greatest Manufacturer* (New York: McGraw-Hill, 2003), 162, describes an encounter when an IT person shared a system design flowchart with Mikio Kitano, the head of Toyota's largest industrial complex. His response was, "At Toyota we do not make information systems. We make cars. Show me the process of making cars and how the information system supports that."

5.   Steve Lohr, "Little Benefit Seen So Far in Electronic Patient Records," *New York Times*, November 15, 2009, reported that a new study of thousands of hospitals to understand the impact of electronic medical records in such key areas as length of stay showed differences that were "really, really marginal," as stated by Dr. Ashish K. Jha, an assistant professor at the Harvard School of Public Health, who headed the study. David U. Himmelstein, *The American Journal of Medicine*, November 20, 2009, studied 4,000 hospitals over five years and states that such bureaucratic actions as "coding and other reimburse-

ment-driven documentation might take precedence over efficiency and the encouragement of clinical parsimony."

6. The same has traditionally applied to Toyota. Liker, *The Toyota Way*, 5. Matthew E. May and Kevin Roberts, *The Elegant Solution: Toyota's Formula for Mastering Innovation* (New York: Free Press, 2006), 88, describes three parts of Toyota's "field approach" to learning to see what the customer values, based on *genchi genbutsu* (or "go and see"): "Observe—watch the customer," "Infiltrate—become the customer," and "Collaborate—involve the customer." The authors explain, using examples, how these are increasingly applied by a range of other companies.

7. Sam Walton and John Huey, *Sam Walton: Made in America* (New York: Doubleday, 1992), 128.

8. Bill Brubaker, "Low-Fare and Hoping: Delta's Pricing Move Simplifies Rates but Leads Carriers in a Risky Direction," *Washington Post* (January 9, 2005): F1, F8.

9. I am grateful to Don Garrity, president and founder of the Garrity Tool Company, for providing this statement and the information in this and the subsequent paragraph about his company's approach and performance during the downturn.

10. Almquist, Bovet, and Heaton, *Collaborative Customer Relationship Management*, 120, draws on research in explaining that "trust can have positive results on customer loyalty."

11. Susan Ganz, CEO of Lion Brothers, provided this information and made this statement during an interview with the author and provided this insight into the company's lean innovation efforts.

12. Drew Greenblatt, CEO of Marlin Wire, made these statements during an interview with the author.

13. Drew Greenblatt provided this information, including the products it creates for companies like Caterpillar, Boeing, or Toyota that support this smoother, leaner way of operating that reduces waste and helps to mitigate sources of lag. He explained that repeat customers are not nearly as concerned about the price of his products after becoming familiar with the great savings they will help create.

14. Almquist, Bovet, and Heaton, *Collaborative Customer Relationship Management*, 120, supports this premise that more innovative solutions will require a progressive track record of collaborative success, stating that "individualism also demands more trust by customers due to the higher risk for an individual when buying a customized product as compared to buying a proven standard solution."

15. Lindsay Chappell, "Toyota Forgoes Layoffs Despite Plant Closings," *Financial Week*, September 8, 2008, provides information on Toyota's approach to keeping workers on the job despite its plant shutdown.

16. Stephen A. Ruffa, *Going Lean: How the Best Companies Apply Lean Manufacturing Principles to Shatter Uncertainty, Drive Innovation, and Maximize Profits* (New York: AMACOM, 2008), 58.

17. Drew Greenblatt, CEO of Marlin Wire, made these statements in this and the subsequent paragraph during an interview with the author.

18. Hanah Cho, "Productivity Rises," *Chicago Tribune*, November 6, 2009, provides these figures.

19. Joe Barrett, "Manufacturers Get Top Talent for Hard-to-Fill Jobs," *Wall Street Journal*, May 30, 2009, describes how companies like Marlin Wire were able to take advantage of the recession and hire top talent.

20. I am grateful to Brent Edmisten at Cessna for providing this information on Cessna's expansion of COEs during the downturn.

21. Womack, Jones, and Roos, *The Machine That Changed the World*, 30, provides insights on repairs drivers could do themselves.

Chapter 10

1. Lindsay Chappell, "Toyota Forgoes Layoffs Despite Plant Closings," *Financial Week*, September 8, 2008.

2. Frank Ahrens and Peter Whoriskey, "Toyota President Apologizes Under Fire of US Officials," *Washington Post*, February 25, 2010, quotes Akio Toyoda, president of Toyota, describing the reason for its massive recall, stating that "Toyota has, for the past few years, been expanding its business rapidly." He further stated, "Quite frankly, I fear the pace at which we have grown may have been too quick."

3. This quote is contained in Alan Ohnsman, "Toyota May Cut US Payrolls as Unsold Autos Pile Up," Bloomberg.com, December 23, 2008. Firms like Southwest Airlines, Walmart, and others seem to have done well at building in capabilities and strategies that respond to both upward and downward shifts; each continued to advance even in these severe conditions.

4. These concerns were raised to the author by Dr. Michael Galiazzo, president of Maryland's Regional Manufacturing Institute, who has decades of experience in community college leadership. He further noted that "lean dynamics applied to learning organizations would produce greater value for students at a lower cost. Public policymak-

ers should rally for this. . . . If I were a college or university president, I would call up 20 manufacturers who have embraced competitive principles and practices and invite them to systemically change the way we create value for the student. I would also have them endorse such radical change. Finally, I would schedule time with legislators to report on the results."

5. L. Kohn, J. Corrigan, and M. Donaldson, *To Err Is Human: Building a Safer Health System* (Washington, DC: Institute of Medicine, National Academy Press, 2000), 1, details the extent and impact of medical errors and provides data on the number of deaths per year.

Appendix A

1. This figure was first introduced in *The Manufacturing Affordability Development Program: A Structured Approach to Rapidly Improved Affordability*, Final Report, Washington, DC: The Naval Air Systems Command and The Joint Strike Fighter Program Office, July 1996; the categories identified to the right of the figure are some examples of the focus areas identified within this report; therefore, they logically might be seen as potential focal points.

Appendix B

1. Taiichi Ohno, *The Toyota Production System*, (Portland, Productivity Press, 1988), 8–9, makes this statement and describes this different way of looking at profit.

2. This chart was first displayed in Stephen A. Ruffa, *Going Lean: How the Best Companies Apply Lean Manufacturing Principles to Shatter Uncertainty, Drive Innovation, and Maximize Profits* (New York: AMACOM, 2008), 216. The supporting data comes from Alfred Sloan, *My Years with General Motors*, 214.

3. This chart was first displayed in Ruffa, *Going Lean*, 217, in which the data calculations are included. The supporting data comes from Alfred Sloan, *My Years with General Motors*, 214.

INDEX

About the Author

Stephen A. Ruffa is an aerospace engineer, a Shingo Prize–winning au-thor, and the originator of the concept of lean dynamics. His distinctive observations are framed by a quarter century of background engaged in supporting many of the Defense Department's dynamic needs—from the design, manufacture, test, and repair of cutting-edge aircraft, to projects ensuring the availability of critical supplies for wartime de-mand surges. His joint government-industry study of lean manufac-turing tools and practices across seventeen aerospace producers, together with his experience with implementing business improve-ment initiatives and his research on today's leading firms, gives him the unique perspective that made this project possible. He is the au-thor of *Going Lean: How the Best Companies Apply Lean Manufactur-ing Principles to Shatter Uncertainty, Drive Innovation, and Maximize Profits* (AMACOM, 2008), and is coauthor of *Breaking the Cost Barrier: A Proven Approach to Managing and Implementing Lean Manufacturing* (John Wiley & Sons, 2000). He provides consulting and other assis-tance to organizations seeking to apply lean dynamics through his company, Lean Dynamics Research, LLC, where he can be reached at www.leandynamics.net.